The Mother Tongue
Student Workbook 2
Answer Key

By
Amy M. Edwards and
Christina J. Mugglin

BLUE SKY DAISIES

The Mother Tongue Student Workbook 2 Answer Key
By Amy M. Edwards and Christina J. Mugglin © 2014

Exercises taken from *The Mother Tongue: Book II*
by George Lyman Kittredge, Sarah Louise Arnold © 1901, 1908 and *The Mother Tongue: Adapted for Modern Students* by Amy M. Edwards and Christina J. Mugglin © 2014.

This answer key accompanies *The Mother Tongue Student Workbook 2*
by Amy M. Edwards and Christina J. Mugglin © 2014.

Published by Blue Sky Daisies
blueskydaisies.net

Cover design: © Blue Sky Daises 2021
ISBN-13: 978-0-9905529-4-9
ISBN-10: 0990552942

THE MOTHER TONGUE
Adapted for Modern Students
STUDENT WORKBOOK 2 ANSWER KEY

This book contains answers to the exercises from *The Mother Tongue: Adapted for Modern Students* which are also contained in the *The Mother Tongue Student Workbook 2.*

Nearly all of the exercises in *The Mother Tongue* are taken from great English writers of centuries past. Where possible, we have supplied the source for many of the sentences and passages used for practice exercises in *The Mother Tongue Book II.* In some instances, Kittredge and Arnold adapted quotations slightly, so they are not always exactly quoted from the original.

We have endeavored to record accurate answers to all of the grammar exercises in *The Mother Tongue Student Workbook 2,* however our efforts are constrained by our humanness. As Pope wrote, "To err is human; to forgive, divine." We beg your forgiveness for any errors you discover. You may contact us and let us know at blueskydaisies.net.

Amy M. Edwards
Christina J. Mugglin
2015

Table of Contents

Chapter 76: Comparison of Adjectives, Part 1

There are no written exercises for chapter 76.

Chapter 77: Comparison of Adjectives, Part 2

I.

Students were instructed to write in three columns the following adjectives in the three degrees of comparison:

	POSITIVE	COMPARATIVE	SUPERLATIVE
1. bright	bright	brighter	brightest
2. lowly	lowly	lowlier	lowliest
3. tall	tall	taller	tallest
4. smooth	smooth	smoother	smoothest
5. rough	rough	rougher	roughest
6. quick	quick	quicker	quickest
7. nimble	nimble	nimbler	nimblest
8. fierce	fierce	fiercer	fiercest
9. black	black	blacker	blackest
10. able	able	abler	ablest
11. subtle	subtle	subtler	subtlest
12. crazy	crazy	crazier	craziest
13. mad	mad	madder	maddest
14. sane	sane	saner	sanest
15. muddy	muddy	muddier	muddiest
16. wet	wet	wetter	wettest
17. dry	dry	drier	driest
18. red	red	redder	reddest
19. sad	sad	sadder	saddest
20. humble	humble	humbler	humblest

II.

Students were asked to circle the adjectives in the comparative or superlative degree. They are in bold print here. They were to also underline the substantive and write the positive degree on the line.

1. He was a **bigger** <u>boy</u> than I. **big**

2. They were some of the **choicest** <u>troops</u> of his whole army. **choice** *(Daniel Defoe (1660-1731),* The Life of Colonel Jack)

3. The <u>town</u> is one of the **neatest** in England. **neat**

4. <u>Life</u> is **dearer** than the golden ore. **dear** *(William Collins (1721-1759), "Hassan, or, The Camel-Driver")*

5. Byron was, at his death, but a <u>year</u> **younger** than Burns. **young** *(Thomas Carlyle (1795-1881),* Robert Burns)

6. On the **highest** <u>part</u> of the mountain is an old fortress. **high** *(Thomas Gray (1716-1771), "Letter to His Mother")*

7. The storm of passion insensibly subsided into **calmer** <u>melancholy</u>. <u>**calm**</u> *(Edward Gibbon (1737-1794), Memoirs of My Life)*

8. The **sternest** sum <u>total</u> of all worldly misfortunes is death. <u>**stern**</u> *(Thomas Carlyle (1795-1881), Robert Burns)*

9. Her <u>astonishment</u> now was **greater** than ever. <u>**great**</u> *(Fanny Burney (1752-1840), Cecilia: Or Memoirs of an Heiress)*

10. The <u>air</u> grew **colder** and **colder**; the <u>mist</u> became **thicker** and **thicker**; the <u>shrieks</u> of the sea fowl **louder** and **louder**. <u>**cold**</u>, <u>**thick**</u>, <u>**loud**</u> *(Susan Ferrier (1782-1854), The Inheritance)*

III.
Students were asked to write sentences for each form (positive, comparative, and superlative) of the following adjectives. The three forms are given. Students' sentences will vary. Check to be sure they have used the adjectives properly.

1. fast, faster, fastest
2. pure, purer, purest
3. low, lower, lowest
4. clumsy, clumsier, clumsiest
5. high, higher, highest
6. large, larger, largest
7. brown, browner, brownest
8. ragged, raggeder, raggedest
9. cross, crosser, crossest
10. deep, deeper, deepest
11. cheery, cheerier, cheeriest
12. merry, merrier, merriest
13. short, shorter, shortest
14. hungry, hungrier, hungriest
15. quiet, quieter, quietest
16. green, greener, greenest
17. manly, manlier, manliest
18. noble, nobler, noblest
19. severe, severer, severest
20. handsome, handsomer, handsomest. People commonly say: handsome, more handsome, most handsome
21. lovely, lovelier, loveliest

Chapter 78: Comparison of Adjectives, Part 3

Students were instructed to underline the adjectives in the comparative degree and circle the adjectives in the superlative degree, which are shown in bold below.

1. The evening was <u>more</u> <u>calm</u> and <u>lovely</u> than any that yet had smiled upon our voyage. *(Thomas Moore (1779-1852),* The Epicurean*)*

2. The environs are **most beautiful**, and the village itself is one of the **prettiest** I ever saw. *(William Cowper (1731-1800), "Letter to Lady Hesketh")*

3. Example is always <u>more</u> <u>efficacious</u> than precept. *(Samuel Johnson (1709-1784),* The History of Rasselas, Prince of Abyssinia: A Tale*)*

4. The Edinburgh scholars of that period were <u>more</u> <u>noted</u> for clearness of head than for warmth of heart. *(Thomas Carlyle (1795-1881),* Robert Burns*)*

5. Nothing could be <u>more</u> <u>bleak</u> and <u>saddening</u> than the appearance of this lake. *(Thomas Moore (1779-1852),* The Epicurean*)*

6. The country became <u>rougher</u>, and the people <u>more</u> <u>savage</u>.

7. He sat down with a **most gloomy** countenance. *(Jane Austen (1775-1817),* Mansfield Park*)*

8. The Caliph remained in the **most violent** agitation. *(William Beckford (1760-1844),* The History of Caliph Vathek*)*

9. A <u>more</u> <u>extraordinary</u> incident has seldom happened.

10. The wind was even <u>more</u> <u>boisterous</u> than usual.

11. The **most elaborate** preparations had been made.

12. The garret windows and housetops were so crowded with spectators that I thought in all my travels I had not seen a <u>more</u> <u>populous</u> place. *(Jonathan Swift (1667-1745),* Gulliver's Travels*)*

Chapter 79: Comparison of Adjectives, Part 4

Students were instructed to underline the comparatives and circle the superlatives, which are shown in bold below.

1. He walked off without <u>further</u> ceremony. *(Jane Austen (1775-1817),* Mansfield Park*)*

2. A friend in the court is <u>better</u> than a penny in purse. *(William Shakespeare (1564-1616),* Second Part of Henry IV*)*

3. Caesar has been called the **foremost** man of all this world. *(Reference to William Shakespeare's (1564-1616),* Julius Caesar*)*

4. The inquisitive prince passed **most** of his nights on the summit of his tower. *(William Beckford (1760-1844),* The History of Caliph Vathek*)*

5. I must confess your offer is the **best**. *(William Shakespeare (1564-1616),* Taming of the Shrew*)*

6. The **worst** minds have often something of good principle in them. *(Sir Walter Scott (1771-1832),* Quentin Durward*)*

7. So doth the <u>greater</u> glory dim the less. *(William Shakespeare (1564-1616),* The Merchant of Venice*)*

8. This island was at a <u>greater</u> distance than I expected, and I did not reach it in less than five hours. *(Jonathan Swift (1667-1745),* Gulliver's Travels*)*

9. There are two or three <u>more</u> pens in the box.

10. I ne'er had <u>worse</u> luck in my life! *(William Shakespeare (1564-1616),* All's Well That Ends Well*)*

11. Lead the way without any <u>more</u> talking. *(William Shakespeare (1564-1616),* The Tempest*)*

12. He grows <u>worse</u> and <u>worse</u>. *(William Shakespeare (1564-1616),* Macbeth*)*

13. I said an <u>elder</u> soldier, not a <u>better</u>. *(William Shakespeare (1564-1616),* Julius Caesar*)*

14. Orlando approached the man and found it was his brother, his <u>elder</u> brother. *(William Shakespeare (1564-1616),* As You Like It*)*

15. Present fears are <u>less</u> than horrible imaginings. *(William Shakespeare (1564-1616),* Macbeth*)*

16. That is Antonio, the duke's **eldest** son. *(William Shakespeare (1564-1616),* All's Well That Ends Well*)*

17. A sad tale's **best** for winter. *(William Shakespeare (1564-1616),* A Winter's Tale*)*

18. To fear the **worst** oft cures the <u>worse</u>. *(William Shakespeare (1564-1616),* Troilus and Cressida*)*

19. The bird is perched on the **topmost** bough.

20. My title's good, and <u>better</u> far than his. *(William Shakespeare (1564-1616),* Third Part of Henry VI*)*

21. I have three daughters; the **eldest** is eleven. *(William Shakespeare (1564-1616),* A Winter's Tale*)*

22. To weep is to make <u>less</u> the depth of grief. *(William Shakespeare (1564-1616),* Third Part of Henry VI*)*

23. He has his health, and <u>ampler</u> strength, indeed,
    Than **most** have of his age. *(William Shakespeare (1564-1616),* A Winter's Tale*)*

24. I will use my **utmost** skill in his recovery. *(William Shakespeare (1564-1616),* Pericles*)*

25. Brutus' love to Caesar was no <u>less</u> than his. *(William Shakespeare (1564-1616),* Julius Caesar*)*

26. My **utmost** efforts were fruitless.

27. We cannot defend the <u>outer</u> fortifications.

Chapter 80: Comparison of Adjectives, Part 5

There are no written exercises for chapter 80.

Chapter 81: Comparison of Adverbs

There are no written exercises for chapter 81.

Chapter 82: Irregular Comparison of Adverbs

Students were instructed to label adverbs with Adv and underline the word it modifies. The adverbs are identified below with (Adv) following the word and the word it modifies is underlined. If the adverb is capable of comparison, students were asked to write its three degrees on the line. The three degrees are given below. If the adverb is not capable of comparison, students should give reasons why.

1. Youth seldom (**Adv**) <u>thinks</u> of dangers.   <u>seldom, seldomer, seldomest</u> *(Sir Walter Scott (1771-1832),* Quentin Durward*)*

2. To every man upon this earth
   Death <u>cometh</u> soon (**Adv**) or late (**Adv**).   <u>soon, sooner, soonest; late, later, latest</u> *(Lord Thomas Macaulay (1800-1859), "Horatius at the Bridge")*

3. So the days <u>passed</u> peacefully (**Adv**) away.   <u>peacefully, more peacefully, most peacefully</u> *(William Black (1841-1898),* Kilmeny*)*

4. It <u>would</u> ill (**Adv**) <u>become</u> me to boast of anything. <u>ill, worse, worst</u> *(Edmund Burke (1729-1797), "A Letter to a Noble Lord")*

5. Delvile eagerly (**Adv**) <u>called</u> to the coachman to drive up to the house, and anxiously (**Adv**) <u>begged</u> Cecilia to sit still.   <u>eagerly, more eagerly, most eagerly; anxiously, more anxiously, most anxiously</u> *(Fanny Burney (1752-1840),* Cecilia: Or Memoirs of an Heiress*)*

6. They <u>came</u> again (**Adv**) and again (**Adv**), and were every time more welcome than before.   <u>Again *is not capable of comparison.*</u> *(Samuel Johnson (1709-1784),* The History of Rasselas, Prince of Abyssinia: A Tale*)*

7. Perhaps this awkwardness <u>will wear</u> off hereafter (**Adv**).   <u>Hereafter *is not capable of comparison.*</u> *(William Cowper (1731-1800), "Letter to Lady Hesketh")*

8. And he, God wot, <u>was forced</u> to stand
   Oft (**Adv**) for his right with blade in hand.   <u>oft, more oft, most oft</u> *(Sir Walter Scott (1771-1832), "Lady of the Lake")*

9. He <u>heard</u> a laugh full (**Adv**) <u>musical</u> aloft (**Adv**).   <u>full, fuller, fullest; aloft, more aloft, most aloft</u> *(John Keats (1795-1821), "Isabella")*

10. The following morning Gertrude <u>arose</u> early (**Adv**).   <u>early, earlier, earliest</u> *(Susan Ferrier (1782-1854),* The Inheritance*)*

11. She <u>walks</u> too (**Adv**) fast (**Adv**), and <u>speaks</u> too (**Adv**) fast (**Adv**). <u>*Too is not capable of comparison;* fast, faster, fastest</u>

12. The seamen spied a rock within half a cable's length of the ship, but the wind was so (**Adv**) <u>strong</u> that we <u>were driven</u> directly (**Adv**) upon it, and immediately (**Adv**) <u>split</u>. <u>*So is not capable of comparison;* directly, more directly, most directly; immediately, more immediately, most immediately</u> *(Jonathan Swift (1667-1745),* Gulliver's Travels)

13. Was that the king that <u>spurred</u> his horse so (**Adv**) hard (**Adv**)? <u>*So is not capable of comparison;* hard, harder, hardest</u> *(William Shakespeare (1564-1616),* Love's Labour Lost)

14. "We <u>know</u> each other well (**Adv**)."
    "We do, and long <u>to know</u> each other worse (**Adv**)." <u>well, better, best; ill, worse, worst</u> *(William Shakespeare (1564-1616),* Troilus and Cressida)

15. He <u>came</u> too (**Adv**) late (**Adv**); the ship was under sail. <u>*Too is not capable of comparison;* late, later, latest</u> *(William Shakespeare (1564-1616),* The Merchant of Venice)

16. How (**Adv**) slow (**Adv**) this old moon <u>wanes</u>! <u>*How is not capable of comparison;* slow, slower, slowest</u> *(William Shakespeare (1564-1616),* A Midsummer Night's Dream)

17. Your judgment is absolutely (**Adv**) <u>correct</u>. <u>absolutely, more absolutely, most absolutely</u>

18. The tide <u>rose</u> higher (**Adv**) and higher (**Adv**). <u>high, higher, highest</u>

19. He <u>swims</u> energetically (**Adv**) but slowly (**Adv**). <u>energetically, more energetically, most energetically; slowly, more slowly, most slowly</u>

20. The courtiers were all (most magnificently) (**Adv**) <u>clad</u>. <u>magnificently, more magnificently, most magnificently</u> *(Jonathan Swift (1667-1745),* Gulliver's Travels)

Chapter 83: Use of Comparative and Superlative

I.

Students were asked to make sentences using the following adjectives and adverbs correctly. Answers will vary. Check to be sure that sentences make sense and properly use the adjective or adverb.

better
best
sooner
most agreeable
nimbler
nimblest
most
more
quicker
quickest
smallest
smaller
most interesting
slower
slowest
more accurate
most accurate

II.
Students were instructed to analyze the sentences that they have made in Exercise I.

III.
Students were instructed to fill in the blanks with adjectives or adverbs in the comparative or the superlative degree as the meaning requires.

1. Tom and I are friends. Indeed he is the (*better* or *best*) __**best**__ friend I have.
2. Which is the (*more* or *most*) ____**more**____ studious of your two sisters?
3. Both generals are brave, but the *old*__**er**___ is of course the (*more* or *most*) __**more**_ experienced of the two.
4. Of all the men in our company I think the very *brave*_**st**__ was Corporal Jackson.
5. Texas is the *large*__**st**_ of the United States.
6. Which is *large*__**r**_, Chicago or Philadelphia?
7. Mention the *large*_**st**_ city in the world.
8. I don't know which I like (*better* or *best*) __**better**__, history or arithmetic.
9. Which do you like (*better* or *best*) __**best**__, history, arithmetic, or reading?
10. I like history (*better* or *best*)_**better**_ than anything else.
11. Of all my studies I like history (*better* or *best*) __**best**__ .
12. Which is the *heavi*_**er**___, a pound of feathers or a pound of gold?
13. Which is the *heavi*__**est**__, a pound of feathers, a pound of lead, or a pound of gold?
14. Jane is the *tall*_**est**_ of the family.

IV.
Students were instructed to compare the following adverbs by writing the comparative and superlative degree.

1. soon, sooner, soonest
2. often, oftener, oftenest. People commonly say: often, more often, most often
3. badly, worse, worst
4. well, better, best
5. noisily, more noisily, most noisily,
6. merrily, more merrily, most merrily
7. far, farther, farthest
8. much, more, most
9. furiously, more furiously, most furiously

V.
Students were instructed to use the superlative of each adverb in IV in a sentence of their own. Answers will vary.

Chapter 84: Demonstrative Pronouns and Adjectives

Students were instructed to write twenty sentences, each containing a demonstrative (*this*, *that*, *these*, or *those*). They were also to examine each sentence, and write whether they have used the demonstrative as a substantive pronoun (subject or object) or as a limiting adjective (adjectively).

Answers will vary.

Chapter 85: Inflection of Demonstratives

I.
Students were instructed to underline each demonstrative in the sentences below and to fill in the chart, identifying if each demonstrative is a pronoun or adjective and singular or plural. If it is a pronoun, they were to give its case.

	PRONOUN (PRO) OR ADJECTIVE (ADJ)?	NUMBER (S/P)	NOMINATIVE (N), OBJECTIVE (O), OR GENITIVE (G) CASE?
1. <u>This</u> is the whole truth.	Pro	S	N
2. <u>This</u> apple is sour.	Adj	S	-
3. <u>These</u> men are brave.	Adj	P	-
4. <u>That</u> is a strange fish.	Pro	S	N
5. <u>That</u> story is false.	Adj	S	-
6. Are you sure of <u>that</u>?	Pro	S	O
7. John told me <u>this</u>.	Pro	S	O
8. <u>These</u> are facts.	Pro	P	N

II.
Students were instructed to underline the demonstratives below, and to label those used substantively (as a subject or object) with S and those used adjectively (as a limiting adjective) with Adj.

1. <u>These</u> (**Adj**) thoughts did not hinder him from sleeping soundly. *(Thomas Hughes (1822-1896)*, Tom Brown at Oxford*)*

2. <u>These</u> (**S**) are Clan-Alpine's warriors true. *(Sir Walter Scott (1771-1832), "Lady of the Lake")*

3. Loth as they were, <u>these</u> (**Adj**) gentlemen had nothing for it but to obey. *(William Makepeace Thackeray (1811-1863)*, The Tremendous Adventures of Major Gahagan*)*

4. "Major Buckley," I said, "What horse is <u>that</u> (**S**)?" *(Henry Kingsley (1830-1876)*, The Recollections of Geoffrey Hamlyn*)*

5. Nor yet for <u>this</u> (**S**), even as a spy,
   Hadst thou, unheard, been doomed to die. *(Sir Walter Scott (1771-1832), "Lady of the Lake")*

6. Ill with King James's mood <u>that</u> (**Adj**) day
   Suited gay feast and minstrel lay. *(Sir Walter Scott (1771-1832), "Lady of the Lake")*

7. <u>That</u> (**Adj**) horse's history would be worth writing. *(Henry Kingsley (1830-1876)*, The Recollections of Geoffrey Hamlyn*)*

8. All <u>this</u> (**S**) was meant to be as irritating as possible. *(Henry Kingsley (1830-1876)*, The Recollections of Geoffrey Hamlyn*)*

9. <u>These</u> (**Adj**) fertile plains, <u>that</u> (**Adj**) softened vale,
   Were once the birthright of the Gael. *(Sir Walter Scott (1771-1832), "Lady of the Lake")*

10. Many hundred large volumes have been published upon <u>this</u> (**Adj**) controversy. *(Jonathan Swift (1667-1745)*, Gulliver's Travels*)*

11. What a good old man <u>that</u> (**S**) is! *(Henry Kingsley (1830-1876)*, The Recollections of Geoffrey Hamlyn*)*

12. <u>That</u> (**S**) absolves me from any responsibility. *(Henry Kingsley (1830-1876),* The Recollections of Geoffrey Hamlyn*)*

13. Jim will be sorry to hear of <u>this</u> (**S**). *(Henry Kingsley (1830-1876),* The Recollections of Geoffrey Hamlyn*)*

14. To hear <u>this</u> (**Adj**) beautiful voice after so long a silence — to find <u>those</u> (**Adj**) calm, dark, friendly eyes regarding him — bewildered him, or gave him courage, he knew not which. *(William Black (1841-1898),* Sunrise*)*

15. <u>This</u> (**Adj**) murderous chief, <u>this</u> (**Adj**) ruthless man,
    <u>This</u> (**Adj**) head of a rebellious clan,
    Hath led thee safe, through watch and ward,
    Far past Clan-Alpine's outmost guard. *(Sir Walter Scott (1771-1832), "Lady of the Lake")*

16. <u>Those</u> (**S**) are terrible questions.

17. <u>These</u> (**S**) were the strong points in his favor. *(Henry Kingsley (1830-1876),* The Hillyers and the Burtons: A Story of Two Families*)*

18. I'll fill <u>these</u> (**Adj**) dogged spies with false reports. *(William Shakespeare (1564-1616),* King John*)*

19. <u>These</u> (**Adj**) soldiers are Danes, <u>those</u> (**S**) are Swedes.

20. Can you hesitate long between <u>this</u> (**S**) and <u>that</u> (**S**)?

Chapter 86: Indefinite Pronouns and Adjectives

Students were instructed to parse the indefinite pronouns, nouns, and adjectives, and to write each word on the line provided, identify it, and tell what part of speech it is in the sentence. The first one was done for the student.

1. They talked about <u>each other's</u> books for hours. **each other's: indefinite compound pronoun, genitive adjective modifying** *books*
2. <u>Some</u> war, <u>some</u> plague, <u>some</u> famine they foresee. **some: indefinite adjective, modifying** *war, plague, famine* (*Alexander Pope (1688-1744), Essay on Morals*)
3. The two armies encountered <u>one another</u> at Towton Field, near Tadcaster. No <u>such</u> battle had been seen in England since the fight of Senlac. **one another: indefinite compound pronoun, direct object; such: indefinite adjective, modifying** *battle* (*John Richard Green (1837-1883),* History of the English People)
4. The morning was raw, and a dense fog was over <u>everything</u>. **everything: indefinite noun, object of the preposition** *over* (*Henry Kingsley (1830-1876),* The Recollections of Geoffrey Hamlyn)
5. <u>Some</u> wild young colts were let out of the stockyard. **some: indefinite adjective, modifying** *colts* (*Henry Kingsley (1830-1876),* The Recollections of Geoffrey Hamlyn)
6. They tell <u>one another</u> all they know, and often more too. **one another: indefinite compound pronoun, indirect object** (*Philip Dormer Stanhope, Earl of Chesterfield (1694-1773), "Lord Chesterfield's Letters"*)
7. Bate me <u>some</u> and I will pay you <u>some</u>. **some: indefinite pronoun, direct object** (*William Shakespeare (1564-1616),* Second Part of Henry IV)
8. I do not wish <u>any</u> companion in the world but you. **any: indefinite adjective, modifying** *companion* (*William Shakespeare (1564-1616),* The Tempest)
9. The big round tears coursed <u>one another</u> down his innocent nose. **one another: indefinite compound pronoun; direct object** (*William Shakespeare (1564-1616),* As You Like It)
10. Grace and remembrance be to you <u>both</u>. **both: indefinite adjective; modifying** *you* (*William Shakespeare (1564-1616),* A Winter's Tale)
11. I know it pleaseth <u>neither</u> of us well. **neither: indefinite pronoun, direct object** (*William Shakespeare (1564-1616),* Richard III)
12. <u>Each</u> hurries toward his home. **each: indefinite pronoun, subject** (*William Shakespeare (1564-1616),* Second Part of Henry IV)
13. Gentlemen <u>both</u>, you will mistake <u>each other</u>. **both: indefinite adjective, modifying** *gentlemen;* **each other: indefinite compound pronoun, direct object** (*William Shakespeare (1564-1616),* Henry V)
14. No <u>such</u> apology is necessary. **such: indefinite adjective, modifying** *apology*
15. Does <u>either</u> of you care for this? **either: indefinite pronoun, subject**
16. <u>Mine</u> honor is my life. <u>Both</u> grow in one. **mine: indefinite adjective, modifying** *honor;* **both: indefinite pronoun, subject** (*William Shakespeare (1564-1616),* Richard II)
17. The parcels contained <u>some</u> letters and verses. **some: indefinite adjective, modifying** *letters and verses* (*Lord Byron (1788-1824),* Letters and Journals of Lord Byron)
18. Think you there was ever <u>such</u> a man? **such: indefinite adjective, modifying** *man* (*William Shakespeare (1564-1616),* Antony and Cleopatra)
19. A black day will it be to <u>somebody</u>. **somebody: indefinite nouns, object of the preposition** *to* (*William Shakespeare (1564-1616),* Richard III)
20. Friend, we understand not <u>one another</u>. **one another: indefinite compound pronoun, direct object** (*William Shakespeare (1564-1616),* Troilus and Cressida)

Chapter 87: The Self-Pronouns

Students were instructed to underline all the self-pronouns and write whether it is an intensive or reflexive pronoun.

If it is an intensive pronouns, students were to draw an arrow to the noun or pronoun with which it is in apposition. This is shown in parentheses.

If it is a reflexive pronoun, students were to draw an arrow to the verb or preposition of which it is the object and they were to circle the noun or pronoun to which each refers back. The verb or preposition is shown in parentheses, the noun is shown in bold print.

1. The **people** (abandoned) <u>themselves</u> to despair. **reflexive** (*Daniel Defoe (1660-1731)*, A Journal of the Plague Year)
2. **Jack** sat (by) <u>himself</u> in a corner. **reflexive**
3. **They** have (talked) <u>themselves</u> hoarse. **reflexive**
4. The (men) <u>themselves</u> carried no provisions except a bag of oatmeal. **intensive** (*Sir Walter Scott (1771-1832)*, Tales of a Grandfather)
5. **Envy** shoots at others, and (wounds) <u>herself</u>. **reflexive**
6. (We) <u>ourselves</u> were wrapped up in our furs. **intensive** (*Thomas Gray (1716-1771)*, The Works of Thomas Gray: Letters)
7. **Clifford** (wrapped) <u>himself</u> in an old cloak. **reflexive**
8. (I) <u>myself</u> am to blame for this. **intensive**
9. **I** shall hardly (know) <u>myself</u> in a blue dress. **reflexive**
10. I have not words to express the poor man's thankfulness, neither could (he) express it <u>himself</u>. **intensive** (*Daniel Defoe (1660-1731)*, A Journal of the Plague Year)
11. Every guilty **deed** holds (in) <u>itself</u> the seed of retribution. **reflexive** (*Henry Wadsworth Longfellow (1807-1882)*, "The Masque of Pandora")
12. (Jane) <u>herself</u> opened the door. **intensive**
13. **She** (amused) <u>herself</u> with walking and reading. **reflexive** (*Fanny Burney (1752-1840)*, Cecilia: Or Memoirs of an Heiress)
14. The (story) <u>itself</u> was scarcely credible. **intensive**
15. The lieutenant was presented to (Washington) <u>himself</u>. **intensive**
16. **Nobody** (save) <u>myself</u> so much as turned to look after him. **reflexive** (*Nathaniel Hawthorne (1804-1864)*, "Mosses From an Old Manse")
17. **One** seldom (dislikes) <u>one's self</u>. **reflexive**
18. The (guides) <u>themselves</u> had lost the path. **intensive**
19. The **prisoner** (threw) <u>himself</u> into the sea and swam for the shore. **reflexive**
20. The old (clock) <u>itself</u> looked weary. **intensive**
21. **(You)** (Guard) <u>thyself</u> from false friends. **reflexive**
22. **You** must (prepare) <u>yourself</u> for the worst. **reflexive**
23. **You** cannot (protect) <u>yourselves</u> from wrong. **reflexive**

Chapter 88: Special Uses of the Self-Pronouns

There are no written exercises for this chapter.

Chapter 89: Numerals

Students were to underline each numeral and write in the blank provided whether it is an adjective (cardinal, ordinal, or other), a noun, or an adverb.

1. <u>Twice</u> through the hall the chieftain strode. **adverb** *(Sir Walter Scott (1771-1832), "Lady of the Lake")*
2. <u>Hundreds</u> in this little town are upon the point of starving. **noun** *(William Cowper (1731-1800), "Letter to Joseph Hill")*
3. I have paid you <u>fourfold</u>. **adverb**
4. The <u>third</u> time never fails. **adjective, ordinal**
5. The English lie within <u>fifteen hundred</u> paces of your tents. **adjective, cardinal** *(William Shakespeare (1564-1616), Henry V)*
6. Methought I saw a <u>thousand</u> fearful wrecks. **adjective, cardinal** *(William Shakespeare (1564-1616), Richard III)*
7. The <u>threefold</u> shield protected him. **adjective, other**
8. They shouted <u>thrice</u>; what was the last cry for? **adverb** *(William Shakespeare (1564-1616), Julius Caesar)*
9. Yet <u>thousands</u> still desire to journey on. **noun** *(William Cowper (1731-1800), "The Task")*
10. Byron died in the <u>thirty-seventh</u> year of his age. **adjective, ordinal**
11. This note doth tell me of <u>ten thousand</u> French   **adjective, cardinal**
    That in the field lie slain: of princes, in this number,
    And nobles bearing banners, there lie dead
    <u>One hundred twenty-six</u>: added to these,   **noun**
    Of knights, esquires, and gallant gentlemen,
    <u>Eight thousand and four hundred</u>. **noun** *(William Shakespeare (1564-1616), Henry V)*

Chapter 89: Review Exercise

Students were instructed to analyze the sentences and parse all the substantives.The first sentence was done for them.

Note: In the *Mother Tongue: Adapted for Modern Students* sentence 25 appeared as sentence 3. It has been moved to number 25 in the workbook as it is a more challenging sentence.

```
     V    S    V    DO    (Adv)  Adv
```
1. <u>Will</u> <u>you</u> <u>shake hands (with me) now</u>?
   you: N, M/F, S   hands: O, N, P

2. <u>(**You**) (**S**) Delay (**V**) not (**Adv**)</u>, Caesar!   <u>(**You**) (**S**) Read (**V**) it (**DO**) instantly (**Adv**)</u>!
   You: N, M/F, S   Caesar: N(Vocative), M, S   it: O, N, S *(William Shakespeare (1564-1616),* Julius Caesar*)*

3. <u>(**You**) (**S**) Lay (**V**) thy (**Adj**) finger (**DO**) (on (**P**) thy (**Adj**) lips (**OP**))</u>. (**Adverbial phrase modifying** *lay*)
   You: N, M/F, S   finger: O, N, S   lips: O, N, P *(William Shakespeare (1564-1616),* Troilus and Cressida*)*

4. <u>Have (**V**) you (**S**) ever (**Adv**) had (**V**) [your (**Adj**) house (**S**) burnt (**V**) down (**Adv**)] (**DO**)</u>?
   you: N, M/F, S/P   house: N, N, S

5. <u>Did (**V**) you (**S**) take (**V**) me (**DO**) (for (**P**) Roger Bacon (**OP**))</u>? (**Adverbial phrase modifying** *did take*)
   you: N, M/F, S   Roger Bacon: O, M, S   me: O, M/F, S *(Sir Walter Scott (1771-1832),* Woodstock: Or, The Cavalier*)*

6. <u>What (**Int**), has (**V**) this (**Adj**) thing (**S**) appeared (**V**) again (**Adv**) tonight (**Adv**)</u>?
   thing: N, N, S *(William Shakespeare (1564-1616),* Hamlet*)*

7. <u>Our (**Adj**) neighbor's (**Adj**) big (**Adj**) black (**Adj**) mastiff (**S**) sprang (**V**) (over (**P**) the (**Adj**) fence (**OP**))</u>. (**Adverbial phrase modifying** *sprang*)
   mastiff: N, M/F, S   fence: O, N, S   neighbor's: G, M/F, S

8. <u>Theodore's (**Adj**) cousin (**S**) has (**V**) just (**Adv**) returned (**V**) (from (**P**) Asia (**OP**))</u>.(**Adverbial phrase modifying** *has returned*)
   Theodore's: G, M, S   cousin: N, M/F, S   Asia: O, N, S

9. <u>The (**Adj**) jay's (**Adj**) noisy (**Adj**) chatter (**S**) silenced (**V**) our (**Adj**) talk (**DO**)</u>.
   Jay's: G, M/F, S   chatter: N, N, S   talk: O, N, S

10. <u>The (**Adj**) old (**Adj**) pilot's (**Adj**) skill (**S**) saved (**V**) the (**Adj**) ship (**DO**) (from (**P**) destruction (**OP**))</u>. (**Adverbial phrase modifying** *saved*)
    pilot's: G, M/F, S   skill: N, N, S   ship: O, F, S   destruction: O, N, S

11. <u>I (**S**) owe (**V**) you (**IO**) much (**DO**) already (**Adv**)</u>.
    I: N, M/F, S   you: O, M/F, S/P   much: O, M/F, P

12. <u>They (**S**) shall (**V**) fetch (**V**) thee (**IO**) jewels (**DO**) (from (**P**) the (**Adj**) deep (**OP**))</u>.(**Adverbial phrase modifying** *shall fetch*)
    jewels: O, N, P   deep: O, N, S   they: N, M/F, P   thee: O, M/F, S *(William Shakespeare (1564-1616),* A Midsummer Night's Dream*)*

13. <u>I (**S**) sell (**V**) thee (**IO**) poison (**DO**)</u>; <u>thou (**S**) hast (**V**) sold (**V**) me (**IO**) none (**DO**)</u>.
    I: N, M/F, S   thee: O, M/F, S   poison: O, N, S   thou: N, M/F, S   me: O, M/F, S   none: O, N, S *(William Shakespeare (1564-1616),* Romeo and Juliet*)*

14. **(You) (S)** <u>Sing **(V)** high **(Adv)** the **(Adj)** praise **(DO)** (of **(P)** Denmark's **(Adj)** host **(OP)**)</u>. (**Adjective phrase modifying** *praise*)
    You: N, M/F, S/P   praise: O, N, S   Denmark's: G, F, S   host: O, M/F, S   *(John Sterling (1806-1844), "Alfred the Harper")*

15. <u>Pen **(S)** never **(Adv)** told **(V)** his **(Adj)** mother **(IO)** a **(Adj)** falsehood **(DO)**</u>.
    Pen: N, M, S   mother: O, F, S   falsehood: O, N, S   *(William Makepeace Thackeray (1811-1863),* History of Pendennis)

16. <u>(Last night)</u> (**Adverbial phrase modifying** *showed*) <u>the **(Adj)** very **(Adj)** gods **(S)** showed **(V)** me **(IO)** a **(Adj)** vision **(DO)**</u>.
    gods: N, M, P   me: O, M/F, S   vision: O, N, S   *(William Shakespeare (1564-1616),* Cymbeline*)*

17. <u>He **(S)** strode **(V)** (down **(P)** the **(Adj)** creaking **(Adj)** stair **(OP)**)</u>. (**Adverbial phrase modifying** *strode*)
    He: N, M, S   stair: O, N, S   *(William Makepeace Thackeray (1811-1863),* History of Pendennis)

18. <u>The **(Adj)** ruling **(Adj)** passion **(S)** conquers **(V)** reason **(DO)** still **(Adv)**</u>.
    passion: N, N, S   reason: O, N, S   *(Alexander Pope (1688-1744),* Essay on Morals)

19. <u>Four **(Adj)** seasons **(S)** fill **(V)** the **(Adj)** measure **(DO)** (of **(P)** the **(Adj)** year **(OP)**)</u>. (**Adjective phrase modifying** *measure*)
    seasons: N, N, P   year: O, N, S   measure: O, N, S   *(John Keats (1795-1821), "The Human Seasons")*

20. <u>He **(S)** feels **(V)** the **(Adj)** anxieties **(DO)** (of **(P)** life **(OP)**)</u>. (**Adjective phrase modifying** *anxieties*)
    He: N, M, S   anxieties: O, N, P   life: O, N, S

21. <u>The **(Adj)** long **(Adj)** carpets **(S)** rose **(V)** (along **(P)** the **(Adj)** gusty **(Adj)** floor **(OP)**)</u>. (**Adverbial phrase modifying** *rose*)
    carpets: N, N, P   floor: O, N, S   *(John Keats (1795-1821), "The Eve of St. Agnes")*

22. <u>The **(Adj)** needle **(S)** plies **(V)** its **(Adj)** busy **(Adj)** task **(DO)**</u>.
    needle: N, N, S   its: G, N, S   task: O, N, S   *(William Cowper (1731-1800), "The Task")*

23. <u>I **(S)** spent **(V)** some **(Adj)** time **(DO)** (in **(P)** Holland **(OP)**)</u>. (**Adverbial phrase modifying** *spent*)
    I: N, M/F, S   time: O, N, S   Holland: O, F, S   *(Daniel Defoe (1660-1731),* Memoirs of a Cavalier)

24. <u>Great **(Adj)** offices **(S)** will **(V)** have **(V)** great **(Adj)** talents **(DO)**</u>.
    offices: N, N, P   talents: O, N, P

25. <u>Do **(V)** you **(S)** not **(Adv)** know **(V)** [that **(C)** [every **(Adj)** hard **(Adj)**, cold **(Adj)** word **(DO)** you **(S)** use **(V)**] **(S)** is **(V)** one **(Adj)** stone **(PN)** (on **(P)** a **(Adj)** great **(Adj)** pyramid **(OP)**) (**Adjective clause modifying** *stone*) (of **(P)** useless **(Adj)** remorse **(OP)**)]? **(DO)**</u> (**Adjective clause modifying** *pyramid*)
    you: N, M/F, S   word: O, N, S   you: N, M/F, S   stone: N, N, S   pyramid: O, N, S
    remorse: O, N, S *(Henry Kingsley (1830-1876),* The Hillyers and the Burtons: A Story of Two Families*)*

Chapter 90: Inflection of Verbs — Tense

There are no written exercises for chapter 90.

Chapter 91: Preterite (Past) Tense

Students were instructed to change the present tense verb to preterite past tense in each sentence. The changed verb is shown below and labeled.

1. I **rode** to Hyde Park. **strong**

2. The country **became** disturbed, and nightly meetings of the peasantry **took** place. **strong, strong** (*Charles James Lever (1806-1872), Harry Lorrequer*)

3. Many of the boldest **sunk** beneath the fear of betrayal. **strong** (*Charles James Lever (1806-1872)*, Harry Lorrequer)

4. When Calabressa **called** at the house in Curzon Street he is at once admitted. **weak** (*William Black (1841-1898)*, Sunrise)

5. He **walked** on, his heart full of an audacious joy. **weak** (*William Black (1841-1898)*, Sunrise)

6. Returning to the cottage, he **proceeded** to sweep the hearth and make up the fire. **weak** (*Thomas Hughes (1822-1896)*, Tom Brown at Oxford)

7. Where the remote Bermudas **rode**
   In the Ocean's bosom unespied,
   From a small boat that **rowed** along,
   The listening winds **received** this song. **strong, weak, weak** (*Andrew Marvell (1621-1678), "The Emigrant's Hymn"*)

8. Many fresh streams **ran** to one salt sea. **strong** (*William Shakespeare (1564-1616)*, Henry V)

9. The camels from their keepers **broke**;
   The distant steer **forsook** the yoke. **strong, strong** (*Lord Byron (1788-1824), "The Siege of Corinth"*)

10. Lady Evelyn **was** a tall, somewhat good-looking, elderly lady, who **wore** her silver-white hair in old-fashioned curls. **strong, strong** (*William Black (1841-1898)*, Sunrise)

11. His faded yellow hair **began** to grow thin, and his thread-bare frock coat **hung** limp from sloping shoulders. **strong, strong** (*George Moore (1852-1933)*, Esther Waters)

12. I **wandered** lonely as a cloud. **weak** (*William Wordsworth (1770-1850), "I Wandered Lonely as a Cloud"*)

13. The next morning he **came** down to the breakfast room earlier than **was** his custom, and **saluted** everybody there with great cordiality. **strong, strong, weak** (*William Makepeace Thackeray (1811-1863)*, History of Pendennis)

14. To the belfry, one by one, **hasted** the ringers. **weak** (Hastened is a more common form of this word.) (*Elizabeth Barrett Browning (1806-1861), adapted from "Rhyme of the Duchess May"*)

15. No haughty feat of arms I **told**. **weak** (*Sir Walter Scott (1771-1832), "Rosabelle"*)

16. The senators **meant** to establish Caesar as a king. **weak** (*William Shakespeare (1564-1616)*, Julius Caesar)

17. I **rested** two or three minutes, and then **gave** the boat another shove, and so on, till the sea **was** no higher than my armpits. **weak, strong, strong** (*Jonathan Swift (1667-1745)*, Gulliver's Travels)

18. His heart **jumped** with pleasure as the famous university **came** in view. **weak, strong** (*William Makepeace Thackeray (1811-1863)*, History of Pendennis)

Chapter 92: Preterite (Past) Tense of Strong (Irregular) Verbs

There are no written exercises for this chapter.

Chapter 93: Weak Preterites (Regular Past Tense) in *-ed* or *-d*

Check to be sure students used the preterite (past tense), shown below, in their sentences. Answers will vary.

1. acted
2. governed
3. rushed
4. knocked
5. fished
6. tended
7. told
8. rattled
9. carried
10. delayed
11. fled
12. tried
13. addressed
14. pitched
15. talked
16. experimented
17. described
18. rebelled

Chapter 94: Weak Preterites (Past Tense) in *-t*

There are no written exercises for chapter 94.

Chapter 95: Weak Preterites Without Ending

I.
Check to be sure students use the preterite (past tense), shown below, in their sentences. Answers will vary.

1. bent
2. sold
3. acted
4. reviewed
5. tried
6. spun
7. drank
8. ate
9. carried
10. lost
11. compelled
12. read
13. led
14. trod
15. left
16. worked
17. spent
18. knew
19. set
20. sat
21. lay (recline) or lied (tell a falsehood)
22. laid
23. rent
24. brought
25. reared
26. arose
27. rang
28. broke
29. bound
30. copied
31. spared
32. multiplied
33. caught
34. divided
35. subtracted
36. telegraphed
37. struck
38. ran
39. wrestled
40. blew
41. burst
42. climbed
43. sang
44. began
45. stood
46. understood
47. went
48. changed
49. taught
50. reached
51. split

II.

Students were instructed to double underline all the preterites (past tense verbs), and mark above the verb whether they are weak with W or strong with S. There were also to write the present tense in each case. The verb markings are shown in parentheses following each verb.

When midnight <u>drew</u> (**S**, **draw**) near, and when the robbers from afar <u>saw</u> (**S**, **see**) that no light was burning and that everything <u>appeared</u> (**W**, **appear**) quiet, their captain <u>said</u> (**W**, **say**) to them that he <u>thought</u> (**W**, **think**) that they had run away without reason, telling one of them to go and reconnoitre. So one of them <u>went</u> (**W**, **go**) and <u>found</u> (**S**, **find**) everything quite quiet. He <u>went</u> (**W**, **go**) into the kitchen to strike a light, and, taking the glowing fiery-eyes of the cat for burning coals, he <u>held</u> (**S**, **hold**) a match to them in order to kindle it. But the cat, not seeing the joke, <u>flew</u> (**S**, **fly**) into his face, spitting and scratching. *(Jacob Grimm (1785-1863) and Wilhelm Grimm (1786-1859), "The Bremen Town Musicians")*

III.

Answers will vary. Suggestions are given and marked strong (S) or weak (W).

1. The hunter took careful aim and **fired** (**W**); but the deer **ran** (**S**) away unharmed.
2. A portrait of Mr. Gilbert **hung** (**S**) on the wall.
3. I **asked** (**W**) my companion to lend me his knife.
4. In the distance **shone** (**S**) the lights of the village.
5. The sailor **dove** (**S**) into the sea and **swam** (**S**) to the rescue.
6. The boy **jumped** (**W**) on the burning deck.
7. The kite **sailed** (**W**) majestically into the air.
8. A puff of wind **blew** (**S**) off the boy's cap and it **sailed** (**W**) along the ground. He **ran** (**S**) after it as fast as he could. The faster he **ran** (**S**), the faster the cap **danced** (**W**).
9. The mischievous fellow **tore** (**S**) three leaves out of my book.
10. The maid **filled** (**W**) the bucket with water and **gave** (**S**) it to the thirsty wayfarers.
11. Tom **sat** (**S**) on a rock, fishing patiently.
12. The miser **dug** (**S**) a hole to conceal his treasure.
13. Joe **climbed** (**W**) the tree to get some apples.

Chapter 96: Singular and Plural Verbs

I.
Answers will vary. Suggestions are given and marked singular (S) or plural (P).

1. I **am (S)** sorry to hear of your misfortune.
2. We **play (P)** ball every Saturday afternoon.
3. He **is (S)** the strongest swimmer in the school.
4. They **are (P)** very good friends of mine.
5. It **takes (S)** a great deal of money to build a railroad.
6. John and Tom always **walk (P)** to school together.
7. Birds **fly (P)**; fishes **swim (P)**; snakes **slither (P)**; dogs **trot (P)** on four legs; mankind alone **walks (S)** upright.
8. You **write (P)** so badly that I can hardly read your letter. Your brother **writes (S)** much better.
9. The farmer **sows (S)** the seed; but the sun and the rain **make (P)** it grow.
10. My uncle **gives (S)** me a dollar whenever he **comes (S)** to visit us.
11. Kangaroos **have (P)** very long hind legs.
12. A spider **has (S)** eight legs; a beetle **has (S)** six.
13. My pony **eats (S)** apples out of my hand.
14. The grocer **sells (S)** tea, sugar, salt, and molasses.
15. The company of soldiers **ran (S)** up the hill in the face of the enemy.
16. The grapes **hang (P)** in clusters on the vine.

II.
Students were instructed to underline the subject, double underline the verb, and circle the objects, which are shown in bold print below. They were also to label the subject and verb singular (S) or plural (P). They should notice the subject/verb agreement.

1. He (S) walked (S) off without further **ceremony**. *(Jane Austen (1775-1817),* Mansfield Park*)*
2. A friend (S) in the court is (S) better than a penny in **purse**. *(William Shakespeare (1564-1616),* Second Part of Henry IV*)*
3. Caesar (S) has been called (S) the foremost **man** of all this **world**. *(Reference to William Shakespeare's (1564-1616),* Julius Caesar*)*
4. The inquisitive prince (S) passed (S) **most** of his **nights** on the **summit** of his **tower**. *(William Beckford (1760-1844),* The History of Caliph Vathek*)*
5. I (S) must confess (S) your offer (S) is (S) the best. *(William Shakespeare (1564-1616),* Taming of the Shrew*)*
6. The worst minds (P) have (P) often **something** of good **principle** in **them**. *(Sir Walter Scott (1771-1832),* Quentin Durward*)*
7. So doth (S) the greater glory (S) dim (S) the **less**. *(William Shakespeare (1564-1616),* The Merchant of Venice*)*
8. This island (S) was (S) at a greater **distance** than I (S) expected (S), and I (S) did (S) not reach (S) **it** in less than five **hours**. *(Jonathan Swift (1667-1745),* Gulliver's Travels*)*
9. There are (P) two or three more pens (P) in the **box**.
10. I (S) ne'er had (S) worse **luck** in my **life**! *(William Shakespeare (1564-1616),* All's Well That Ends Well*)*
11. (You) (S) Lead (S) the **way** without any more **talking**. *(William Shakespeare (1564-1616),* The Tempest*)*
12. He (S) grows (S) worse and worse. *(William Shakespeare (1564-1616),* Macbeth*)*
13. I (S) said (S) an elder **soldier**, not a better. *(William Shakespeare (1564-1616),* Julius Caesar*)*
14. Orlando (S) approached (S) the **man** and found (S) it (S) was (S) his **brother**, his elder **brother**. *(William Shakespeare (1564-1616),* As You Like It*)*
15. Present fears (P) are (P) less than horrible imaginings. *(William Shakespeare (1564-1616),* Macbeth*)*

16. <u>That</u> (S) <u><u>is</u></u> (S) Antonio, the duke's eldest son. *(William Shakespeare (1564-1616), All's Well That Ends Well)*
17. A sad <u>tale</u> (S) <u><u>'s</u></u> (S) best for **winter**. *(William Shakespeare (1564-1616), A Winter's Tale)*
18. <u>To fear the worst</u> (S) <u><u>cures</u></u> (S) the **worse**. *(William Shakespeare (1564-1616), Troilus and Cressida)*
19. The <u>bird</u> (S) <u><u>is perched</u></u> (S) on the topmost **bough**.
20. My <u>title</u> (S) <u><u>'s</u></u> (S) good, and better far than his. *(William Shakespeare (1564-1616), Third Part of Henry VI)*
21. <u>I</u> (S) <u><u>have</u></u> (S) three **daughters**; the <u>eldest</u> (S) <u><u>is</u></u> (S) eleven. *(William Shakespeare (1564-1616), A Winter's Tale)*
22. <u>To weep</u> (S) <u><u>is</u></u> (S) to make less the depth of **grief**. *(William Shakespeare (1564-1616), Third Part of Henry VI)*
23. <u>He</u> (S) <u><u>has</u></u> (S) his **health**, and ampler **strength**, indeed,
    Than <u>most</u> (P) <u><u>have</u></u> (P) of his **age**. *(William Shakespeare (1564-1616), A Winter's Tale)*
24. <u>I</u> (S) <u><u>will use</u></u> (S) my utmost **skill** in his **recovery**. *(William Shakespeare (1564-1616), Pericles)*
25. Brutus' <u>love</u> (S) to Caesar <u><u>was</u></u> (S) no less than his. *(William Shakespeare (1564-1616), Julius Caesar)*
26. My utmost <u>efforts</u> (P) <u><u>were</u></u> (P) fruitless.
27. <u>We</u> (P) <u><u>can</u></u> (P) not <u><u>defend</u></u> (P) the outer **fortifications**.

III.
Students were instructed to underline the subject, double underline the verb, and circle the objects, which are shown in bold print below. There were also to label the subject and verb singular (S) or plural (P). They should notice the subject/verb agreement.

1. These <u>thoughts</u> (P) <u><u>did</u></u> (P) not <u><u>hinder</u></u> (P) **him** from **sleeping** soundly. *(Thomas Hughes (1822-1896), Tom Brown at Oxford)*
2. <u>These</u> (P) <u><u>are</u></u> (P) Clan-Alpine's **warriors** true. *(Sir Walter Scott (1771-1832), "Lady of the Lake")*
3. Loth as <u>they</u> (P) <u><u>were</u></u> (P), these <u>gentlemen</u> (P) <u><u>had</u></u> (P) **nothing** for **it** but to obey. *(William Makepeace Thackeray (1811-1863), The Tremendous Adventures of Major Gahagan)*
4. "Major Buckley," <u>I</u> (S) <u><u>said</u></u> (S), "<u>What</u> (S) **horse** <u><u>is</u></u> (S) that?" *(Henry Kingsley (1830-1876), The Recollections of Geoffrey Hamlyn)*
5. Nor yet for **this**, even as a **spy**,
   <u><u>Hadst</u></u> (S) <u>thou</u> (S), unheard, <u><u>been doomed</u></u> (S) to die. *(Sir Walter Scott (1771-1832), "Lady of the Lake")*
6. Ill with King James's **mood** that <u>day</u> (S)
   <u><u>Suited</u></u> gay **feast** and minstrel **lay**. *(Sir Walter Scott (1771-1832), "Lady of the Lake")*
7. That horse's <u>history</u> (S) <u><u>would be</u></u> (S) worth writing. *(Henry Kingsley (1830-1876), The Recollections of Geoffrey Hamlyn)*
8. All <u>this</u> (S) <u><u>was meant</u></u> (S) to be as irritating as possible. *(Henry Kingsley (1830-1876), The Recollections of Geoffrey Hamlyn)*
9. These fertile <u>plains</u> (P), that softened <u>vale</u> (P),
   <u><u>Were</u></u> (P) once the **birthright** of the **Gael**. *(Sir Walter Scott (1771-1832), "Lady of the Lake")*
10. Many hundred large <u>volumes</u> (P) <u><u>have been published</u></u> (P) upon this **controversy**.
11. What a good old man <u>that</u> (S) <u><u>is</u></u> (S)! *(Henry Kingsley (1830-1876), The Recollections of Geoffrey Hamlyn)*
12. <u>That</u> (S) <u><u>absolves</u></u> (S) **me** from any **responsibility**. *(Henry Kingsley (1830-1876), The Recollections of Geoffrey Hamlyn)*
13. <u>Jim</u> (S) <u><u>will be</u></u> (S) sorry to hear of **this**. *(Henry Kingsley (1830-1876), The Recollections of Geoffrey Hamlyn)*
14. To hear this beautiful **voice** after so long a **silence** — to find those calm, dark, friendly **eyes** regarding **him** — <u><u>bewildered</u></u> (S) **him**, or <u><u>gave</u></u> him **courage**, <u>he</u> (S) <u><u>knew</u></u> (S) not which. *(William Black (1841-1898), Sunrise)*

15. This murderous <u>chief</u> (S), this ruthless <u>man</u> (S),
    This <u>head</u> (S) of a rebellious **clan**,
    <u>Hath led</u> (S) **thee** safe, through **watch** and **ward**,
    Far past Clan-Alpine's outmost **guard**. *(Sir Walter Scott (1771-1832), "Lady of the Lake")*

16. <u>Those</u> (P) <u>are</u> (P) terrible **questions**.

17. <u>These</u> (P) <u>were</u> (P) the strong **points** in his **favor**. *(Henry Kingsley (1830-1876),* The Hillyers and the Burtons: A Story of Two Families*)*

18. <u>I</u> (S) <u>'ll fill</u> (S) these dogged **spies** with false **reports**. *(William Shakespeare (1564-1616),* King John*)*

19. These <u>soldiers</u> (P) <u>are</u> (P) Danes, <u>those</u> (P) <u>are</u> (P) Swedes.

20. <u>Can (S/P)</u> <u>you</u> (S/P) <u>hesitate</u> (S/P) long between **this** and **that**?

Chapter 97: Special Rules for the Number of Verbs

There are no written exercises for chapter 97.

Chapter 98: Person of Verbs

I.
Answers will vary. Check to see that the students have written an account about some accident or adventure in both the first and the third person.

What changes have you made in the form of each verb?
The person of the verb was changed.

II.

> When I came to the throne in 1413 A.D., I gave up all my wild ways and tried to rule as a wise king should. Judge Gascoigne was much afraid that he would suffer now for having sent me to prison. But I had a noble mind. I knew that the judge had only done what was right. So after I became king, I treated Judge Gascoigne as a friend, and when he gave up his judgeship it was because he was a very old man. "Still be my judge," I said, "and if I should ever have a son who does wrong, I hope you will punish him as you did me."

What changes have you made in the form of each verb?
Changed the person from third to first.
(Original passage from H. E. Marshall (1867-1941), Our Island Story*)*

III.
Students were instructed to circle the person and number of each of the verbs and verb phrases. Answers are shown in bold below. If the form may belong to more than one person or number, each is bolded. Test your accuracy by using personal pronouns (*I, you, they,* etc.) with each form. Some of the verb forms given are the archaic form. For example, *Thou didst know.* NOTE: Unless an archaic form is given, the key assumes that the student will circle the modern use. (Incorrect choices are greyed out.)

		SINGULAR			PLURAL		
		1st	2nd	3rd	1st	2nd	3rd
1.	found	**1st**	**2nd**	**3rd**	**1st**	**2nd**	**3rd**
2.	didst know		**2nd**				
3.	finds			**3rd**			
4.	acts			**3rd**			
5.	act	**1st**	**2nd**		**1st**	**2nd**	**3rd**
6.	mentions			**3rd**			
7.	sells			**3rd**			
8.	sold	**1st**	**2nd**	**3rd**	**1st**	**2nd**	**3rd**
9.	broughtest		**2nd**				
10.	brings			**3rd**			
11.	bringest		**2nd**				
12.	speak	**1st**	**2nd**		**1st**	**2nd**	**3rd**
13.	spoke	**1st**	**2nd**	**3rd**	**1st**	**2nd**	**3rd**
14.	broke	**1st**	**2nd**	**3rd**	**1st**	**2nd**	**3rd**
15.	endeavors			**3rd**			

The Mother Tongue Student Workbook 2

#		SINGULAR			PLURAL		
		1st	2nd	3rd	1st	2nd	3rd
16.	dives	1st	2nd	**3rd**	1st	2nd	3rd
17.	replied	**1st**	**2nd**	**3rd**	**1st**	**2nd**	**3rd**
18.	puzzled	**1st**	**2nd**	**3rd**	**1st**	**2nd**	**3rd**
19.	utters	1st	2nd	**3rd**	1st	2nd	3rd
20.	knowest	1st	**2nd**	3rd	1st	2nd	3rd
21.	hath	1st	2nd	**3rd**	1st	2nd	3rd
22.	has	1st	2nd	**3rd**	1st	2nd	3rd
23.	canst	1st	**2nd**	3rd	1st	2nd	3rd
24.	can	**1st**	**2nd**	**3rd**	**1st**	**2nd**	**3rd**
25.	is	1st	2nd	**3rd**	1st	2nd	3rd
26.	are	1st	**2nd**	3rd	**1st**	**2nd**	**3rd**
27.	leapest	1st	**2nd**	3rd	1st	2nd	3rd
28.	fight	**1st**	**2nd**	3rd	**1st**	**2nd**	**3rd**
29.	fought	**1st**	**2nd**	**3rd**	**1st**	**2nd**	**3rd**
30.	has spoken	1st	2nd	**3rd**	1st	2nd	3rd
31.	have	**1st**	**2nd**	3rd	**1st**	**2nd**	**3rd**
32.	am	**1st**	2nd	3rd	1st	2nd	3rd
33.	art	1st	**2nd**	3rd	1st	2nd	3rd
34.	were	1st	**2nd**	3rd	**1st**	**2nd**	**3rd**

IV.

Alice looked on with great interest as the King took an enormous memorandum-book out of his pocket, and began writing. A sudden thought struck her, and she took hold of the end of the pencil, which came some way over his shoulder, and began writing for him.

The poor King looked puzzled and unhappy, and struggled with the pencil for some time without saying anything; but Alice was too strong for him, and at last he panted out "My dear! I really *must* get a thinner pencil. I can't manage this one a bit. It writes all manner of things that I don't intend--"

"What manner of things?" said the Queen, looking over the book (in which Alice had put *'The White Knight is sliding down the poker. He balances very badly'*) "That's not a memorandum of *your* feelings!"

There was a book lying near Alice on the table, and while she sat watching the White King (for she was still a little anxious about him, and had the ink all ready to throw over him, in case he fainted again), she turned over the leaves, to find some part that she could read, "---for it's all in some language I don't know," she said to herself. *(Lewis Carroll (1832-1898),* Alice in Wonderland)

looked: third person, singular, preterite (past)
took: third person, singular, preterite (past)
began: third person, singular, preterite (past)
struck: third person, singular, preterite (past)
took: third person, singular, preterite (past)

came: third person, singular, preterite (past)
began: third person, singular, preterite (past)
looked: third person, singular, preterite (past)
struggled: third person, singular, preterite (past)
was: third person, singular, preterite (past)
panted: third person, singular, preterite (past)
writes: third person, singular, present
said: third person, singular, preterite (past)
balances: third person, singular, present
is: third person, singular, present
was: third person, singular, preterite (past)
sat: third person, singular, preterite (past)
was: third person, singular, preterite (past)
had: third person, singular, preterite (past)
fainted: third person, singular, preterite (past)
turned: third person, singular, preterite (past)
is: third person, singular, present
said: third person, singular, preterite (past)

Chapter 99: Personal Endings — Conjugating Verbs

I.

Students were instructed to conjugate the following verbs in the present and the preterite (past) tense. The first one was done for the student. (You may allow your student to conjugate the second person singular "Thou lovest," with the plural form, "You love," since this is the modern convention.)

VERB	PRESENT TENSE		PRETERITE (PAST) TENSE	
	SINGULAR	PLURAL	SINGULAR	PLURAL
love	*love* *lovest* *loves*	*love* *love* *love*	*loved* *lovedst* *loved*	*loved* *loved* *loved*
call	*call* *call* *calls*	*call* *call* *call*	*called* *called* *called*	*called* *called* *called*
answer	*answer* *answer* *answers*	*answer* *answer* *answer*	*answered* *answered* *answered*	*answered* *answered* *answered*
shout	*shout* *shout* *shouts*	*shout* *shout* *shout*	*shouted* *shouted* *shouted*	*shouted* *shouted* *shouted*
examine	*examine* *examine* *examines*	*examine* *examine* *examine*	*examined* *examined* *examined*	*examined* *examined* *examined*
stand	*stand* *stand* *stands*	*stand* *stand* *stand*	*stood* *stood* *stood*	*stood* *stood* *stood*
find	*find* *find* *finds*	*find* *find* *find*	*found* *found* *found*	*found* *found* *found*
bind	*bind* *bind* *binds*	*bind* *bind* *bind*	*bound* *bound* *bound*	*bound* *bound* *bound*
bear	*bear* *bear* *bears*	*bear* *bear* *bear*	*bore* *bore* *bore*	*bore* *bore* *bore*
lose	*lose* *lose* *loses*	*lose* *lose* *lose*	*lost* *lost* *lost*	*lost* *lost* *lost*

VERB	PRESENT TENSE		PRETERITE (PAST) TENSE	
	SINGULAR	PLURAL	SINGULAR	PLURAL
sit	*sit* *sit* *sits*	*sit* *sit* *sit*	*sat* *sat* *sat*	*sat* *sat* *sat*
set	*set* *set* *sets*	*set* *set* *set*	*set* *set* *set*	*set* *set* *set*
lie (to tell a falsehood)	*lie* *lie* *lies*	*lie* *lie* *lie*	*lied* *lied* *lied*	*lied* *lied* *lied*
lay	*lay* *lay* *lays*	*lay* *lay* *lay*	*laid* *laid* *laid*	*laid* *laid* *laid*
burn	*burn* *burn* *burns*	*burn* *burn* *burn*	*burned* *burned* *burned*	*burned* *burned* *burned*
fight	*fight* *fight* *fights*	*fight* *fight* *fight*	*fought* *fought* *fought*	*fought* *fought* *fought*
bring	*bring* *bring* *brings*	*bring* *bring* *bring*	*brought* *brought* *brought*	*brought* *brought* *brought*
catch	*catch* *catch* *catches*	*catch* *catch* *catch*	*caught* *caught* *caught*	*caught* *caught* *caught*
reach	*reach* *reach* *reaches*	*reach* *reach* *reach*	*reached* *reached* *reached*	*reached* *reached* *reached*
spend	*spend* *spend* *spends*	*spend* *spend* *spend*	*spent* *spent* *spent*	*spent* *spent* *spent*
beat	*beat* *beat* *beats*	*beat* *beat* *beat*	*beat* *beat* *beat*	*beat* *beat* *beat*
declare	*declare* *declare* *declares*	*declare* *declare* *declare*	*declared* *declared* *declared*	*declared* *declared* *declared*
read	*read* *read* *reads*	*read* *read* *read*	*read* *read* *read*	*read* *read* *read*

VERB	PRESENT TENSE		PRETERITE (PAST) TENSE	
	SINGULAR	PLURAL	SINGULAR	PLURAL
march	*march* *march* *marches*	*march* *march* *march*	*marched* *marched* *marched*	*marched* *marched* *marched*
charge	*charge* *charge* *charges*	*charge* *charge* *charge*	*charged* *charged* *charged*	*charged* *charged* *charged*
enlarge	*enlarge* *enlarge* *enlarges*	*enlarge* *enlarge* *enlarge*	*enlarged* *enlarged* *enlarged*	*enlarged* *enlarged* *enlarged*
despise	*despise* *despise* *despises*	*despise* *despise* *despise*	*despised* *despised* *despised*	*despised* *despised* *despised*
praise	*praise* *praise* *praises*	*praise* *praise* *praise*	*praised* *praised* *praised*	*praised* *praised* *praised*
honor	*honor* *honor* *honors*	*honor* *honor* *honor*	*honored* *honored* *honored*	*honored* *honored* *honored*
foretell	*foretell* *foretell* *foretells*	*foretell* *foretell* *foretell*	*foretold* *foretold* *foretold*	*foretold* *foretold* *foretold*
prophesy	*prophesy* *prophesy* *prophesies*	*prophesy* *prophesy* *prophesy*	*prophesied* *prophesied* *prophesied*	*prophesied* *prophesied* *prophesied*
enter	*enter* *enter* *enters*	*enter* *enter* *enter*	*entered* *entered* *entered*	*entered* *entered* *entered*
depart	*depart* *depart* *departs*	*depart* *depart* *depart*	*departed* *departed* *departed*	*departed* *departed* *departed*

II.

Students were instructed to write the verbs in the blank provided and circle the number (**S/P**) and person (**1/2/3**) of each verb.

1.	was	S	3		17.	came	P	3
2.	accompanied	S	3			emblazoned	S	3
3.	was	S	3		18.	can be recalled	S	3
4.	art doing	S	2			must go	S	3
5.	mean	S	3		19.	saw	S	3
	think	S	1			played	S	3
	can guess	S	1		20.	have endeavored	S	1
6.	boast	S	2		21.	has furnished	S	3
7.	closes	S	3		22.	ambled	S	3
8.	was	S	1			were walking	P	3
	roared	S	1		23.	held	P	3
	ran	P	3			was	S	3
9.	listens	S	3			lay	P	1
	can hear	S	3		24.	shall weep	S	3
10.	hollowed	S	3			must die	S	2
	carried	S	3		25.	lend	S	2
11.	were filled	P	3		26.	must come	S	2
12.	are masters	P	3			would speak	S	3
13.	is	S	3		27.	should do	P	1
	would speak	S	3		28.	stay	P	1
14.	should unfurl	P	1		29.	are	P	1
15.	thought	S	1					
16.	had departed	P	3					

III.

Students were instructed to conjugate the following verbs in the present tense, giving all three persons and both numbers. They were also to use a pronoun as the subject of each verb. (Note: Students may conjugate the second person singular in the modern usage, which is technically the second person plural form. Although the sample gives the formal second person singular with *thou*, the key will show *you*. Please note, however, that if your student chooses to use *thou*, they must use the *-st* ending.)

Verb	Present Tense	
	Singular	Plural
love	*I love.* *Thou lovest.* *He loves.*	*We love.* *You love.* *They love.*
stand	*I stand.* *You stand.* *He stands.*	*We stand.* *You stand.* *They stand.*
answer	*I answer.* *You answer.* *He answers.*	*We answer.* *You answer.* *They answer.*
compel	*I compel.* *You compel.* *He compels.*	*We compel.* *You compel.* *They compel.*
go	*I go.* *You go.* *He goes.*	*We go.* *You go.* *They go.*
ask	*I ask.* *You ask.* *He asks.*	*We ask.* *You ask.* *They ask.*
fill	*I fill.* *You fill.* *He fills.*	*We fill.* *You fill.* *They fill.*
try	*I try.* *You try.* *He tries.*	*We try.* *You try.* *They try.*
succeed	*I succeed.* *You succeed.* *He succeeds.*	*We succeed.* *You succeed.* *They succeed.*
spend	*I spend.* *You spend.* *He spends.*	*We spend.* *You spend.* *They spend.*
earn	*I earn.* *You earn.* *He earns.*	*We earn.* *You earn.* *They earn.*

VERB	PRESENT TENSE	
	SINGULAR	PLURAL
study	I study. You study. He studies.	We study. You study. They study.
run	I run. You run. He runs.	We run. You run. They run.
rescue	I rescue. You rescue. He rescues.	We rescue. You rescue. They rescue.
play	I play. You play. He plays.	We play. You play. They play.
climb	I climb. You climb. He climbs.	We climb. You climb. They climb.
flee	I flee. You flee. He flees.	We flee. You flee. They flee.
retreat	I retreat. You retreat. He retreats.	We retreat. You retreat. They retreat.
charge	I charge. You charge. He charges.	We charge. You charge. They charge.
descend	I descend. You descend. He descends.	We descend. You descend. They descend.
ride	I ride. You ride. He rides.	We ride. You ride. They ride.
act	I act. You act. He acts.	We act. You act. They act.
smile	I smile. You smile. He smiles.	We smile. You smile. They smile.
laugh	I laugh. You laugh. He laughs.	We laugh. You laugh. They laugh.

VERB	PRESENT TENSE	
	SINGULAR	PLURAL
speed	*I speed.* *You speed.* *He speeds.*	*We speed.* *You speed.* *They speed.*
descry	*I descry.* *You descry.* *He descries.*	*We descry.* *You descry.* *They descry.*
find	*I find.* *You find.* *He finds.*	*We find.* *You find.* *They find.*
bring	*I bring.* *You bring.* *He brings.*	*We bring.* *You bring.* *They bring.*
discover	*I discover.* *You discover.* *He discovers.*	*We discover.* *You discover.* *They discover.*
desire	*I desire.* *You desire.* *He desires.*	*We desire.* *You desire.* *They desire.*
retreat	*I retreat.* *You retreat.* *He retreats.*	*We retreat.* *You retreat.* *They retreat.*
succeed	*I succeed.* *You succeed.* *He succeeds.*	*We succeed.* *You succeed.* *They succeed.*
drink	*I drink.* *You drink.* *He drinks.*	*We drink.* *You drink.* *They drink.*
lead	*I lead.* *You lead.* *He leads.*	*We lead.* *You lead.* *They lead.*
bend	*I bend.* *You bend.* *He bends.*	*We bend.* *You bend.* *They bend.*

IV.

Answers will vary.

Chapter 100: Infinitive

I.
Answers will vary.

II.
Answers will vary. Suggestions are given.

1. Old Carlo was too well trained **to chase** cats.
2. Charles was in such a hurry that he could hardly spare time **to eat** his breakfast.
3. We are taught **to love** our enemies.
4. Gerald rose very early and went down to the brook **to fish** for trout.
5. Little Bo-Peep has lost her sheep,
   And doesn't know where **to find** them. *(Mother Goose Nursery Rhyme)*
6. The fireman was obliged **to jump** from the locomotive to save his life.
7. The careless fellow has forgotten **to shut** the door.
8. Our orders were **to charge** against the enemy at daybreak.
9. Commodore Dewey did not hesitate **to sail** into Manila Bay.
10. The performing bear stood up on his hind legs and began **to dance** clumsily.

III.
The infinitives are underlined below.

1. Lord Craven did me the honor **to inquire** for me by name.
2. Distress at last forced him **to leave** the country.
3. I know not what **to think** of it.
4. Our next care was **to bring** this booty home without meeting with the enemy. *(Daniel Defoe (1660-1731), Memoirs of a Cavalier)*
5. **To see** judiciously requires no small skill in the seer. *(Susan Ferrier (1782-1854), The Inheritance)*
6. The business of his own life is **to dine**.
7. The ladies are **to fling** nosegays; the court poets **to scatter** verses; the spectators are **to be** all in full dress. *(Oliver Goldsmith (1730-1774), Citizen of the World)*
8. Vathek invited the old man **to dine**, and even **to remain** some days in the palace. *(William Beckford (1760-1844), The History of Caliph Vathek)*
9. Earth seemed **to sink** beneath, and heaven above **to fall**. *(John Dryden (1631-1700), "The Cock and the Fox, or the Tale of the Nun's Priest")*

Chapter 101: Participles

Students were instructed to circle the participles which are shown in bold below, and underline the noun or pronoun that it modifies.

1. I see <u>trees</u> **laden** with **ripening** <u>fruit</u>. (*Charlotte Brontë (1816-1855)*, Jane Eyre)
2. In the green churchyard there were <u>cattle</u> tranquilly **reposing** upon the verdant graves. (*Thomas De Quincey (1785-1859)*, Confessions of an English Opium-Eater)
3. The <u>mob</u> came **roaring** out, and thronged the place. (*John Dryden (1631-1700), "The Cock and the Fox," a poem of "The Nun's Priest's Tale"*)
4. The <u>girls</u> sat **weeping** in silence. (*Samuel Johnson (1709-1784)*, The History of Rasselas, Prince of Abyssinia: A Tale)
5. **Asked** for a groat, <u>he</u> gives a thousand pounds. (*Alexander Pope (1688-1744)*, The Sixth Epistle of the First Book of Horace, *Pope actually wrote, "...gives a hundred pounds."*)
6. <u>Edward</u> marched through Scotland at the head of a powerful army, **compelling** all ranks of people to submit to him. (*Sir Walter Scott (1771-1832)*, Tales of a Grandfather)
7. The blackest <u>desperation</u> now gathers over him, **broken** only by red lightnings of remorse. (*Thomas Carlyle (1795-1881)*, Robert Burns)
8. **Arrived** at Athens, soon <u>he</u> came to court. (*John Dryden (1631-1700), "Palamon and Arcite," a poem retelling the "A Knight's Tale"*)
9. Still the <u>vessel</u> went **bounding** onward. (*Nathaniel Hawthorne (1804-1864)*, Tanglewood Tales)
10. **Enchanted** with the whole scene, <u>I</u> lingered on my voyage. (*Thomas Moore (1779-1852)*, The Epicurean)
11. So **saying**, from the pavement <u>he</u> half rose
    Slowly, with pain, **reclining** on his arm,
    And **looking** wistfully with wide blue eyes
    As in a picture. (*Alfred, Lord Tennyson (1809-1892)*, Morte D'Arthur)
12. <u>I</u> went home that evening greatly **oppressed** in my mind, irresolute, and not **knowing** what to do. (*Daniel Defoe (1660-1731)*, A Journal of the Plague Year)
13. Methinks I see <u>thee</u> **straying** on the beach.
14. A <u>mountain</u> stood
    Threatening from high,
    and overlooked the wood.
15. The **wondering** <u>stranger</u> round him gazed. (*Sir Walter Scott (1771-1832), "Lady of the Lake"*)
16. The <u>castaways</u> haunted the shore of the little island, always **straining** their eyes in the vain hope that a ship might show itself on the horizon.
17. <u>Jack</u> said nothing, but stood **looking** quizzically at his cousin.
18. **Hearing** of the disaster, <u>they</u> had come to my assistance.
19. At the first fire, <u>twenty</u> or <u>thirty</u> of the assailants fell **dead** or **wounded**.
20. <u>Egbert</u> stood motionless, **horrified** at the sight.
21. Almost **exhausted**, and **swimming** with the greatest difficulty, <u>Philip</u> reached the pier at last.
22. I found <u>him</u> **hiding** behind a tree.

Chapter 102: Present Participle

There are no written exercises for chapter 102.

Chapter 103: Past Participle of Weak Verbs

I.

1. The farmer sows his seed.
    Preterite The farmer sowed his seed.
    Past Participle The farmer has sown his seed.

2. The maid sets the table.
    Preterite The maid set the table.
    Past Participle The maid has set the table.

3. The dog obeys his master.
    Preterite The dog obeyed his master.
    Past Participle The dog has obeyed his master.

4. The pupil answers the question.
    Preterite The pupil answered the questions.
    Past Participle The pupil has answered the question.

5. The girl reads her book.
    Preterite The girl read her book.
    Past Participle The girl has read the book.

6. He spends his money freely.
    Preterite He spent his money freely.
    Past Participle He has spent his money freely.

7. He feels sorry for his faults.
    Preterite He felt sorry for his faults.
    Past Participle He has felt sorry for his faults.

II.

Give the present, the preterite (past tense), and the past participle of each verb.

	PRESENT	PRETERITE (PAST)	PAST PARTICIPLE
1. quarrel	quarrel	quarreled	quarreled
2. accept	accept	accepted	accepted
3. tell	tell	told	told
4. offer	offer	offered	offered
5. hit	hit	hit	hit
6. drown	drown	drowned	drowned
7. flee	flee	fled	fled
8. start	start	started	started
9. arrive	arrive	arrived	arrived
10. hear	hear	heard	heard
11. convey	convey	conveyed	conveyed
12. sleep	sleep	slept	slept
13. obey	obey	obeyed	obeyed
14. cut	cut	cut	cut
15. delay	delay	delayed	delayed
16. sweep	sweep	swept	swept
17. sell	sell	sold	sold
18. stay	stay	stayed	stayed
19. feel	feel	felt	felt
20. make	make	made	made
21. deal	deal	dealt	dealt
22. beseech	beseech	beseeched	beseeched
23. creep	creep	crept	crept
24. bring	bring	brought	brought
25. shut	shut	shut	shut
26. cast	cast	cast	cast
27. keep	keep	kept	kept
28. lose	lose	lost	lost
29. catch	catch	caught	caught
30. cost	cost	cost	cost
31. leave	leave	left	left

Chapter 104: Past Participle of Strong Verbs

I.

1. Nobody knows the truth of the matter.
   Preterite Nobody **knew** the truth of the matter.
   Past Participle Nobody **has known** the truth of the matter.

2. Henry writes to his mother every day.
   Preterite Henry **wrote** to his mother every day.
   Past Participle Henry **has written** to his mother every day.

3. The arrow strikes the target near the center.
   Preterite The arrow **struck** the target near the center.
   Past Participle The arrow **has struck** the target near the center.

4. The explosion throws down the wall.
   Preterite The explosion **threw** down the wall.
   Past Participle The explosion **has thrown** down the wall.

5. January 1, 1901, begins a new century.
   Preterite January 1, 1901, **began** a new century.
   Past Participle January 1, 1901, **has begun** a new century.

6. The boy stands on the burning deck.
   Preterite The boy **stood** on the burning deck.
   Past Participle The boy **has stood** on the burning deck.

7. A great banquet takes place tonight.
   Preterite A great banquet **took** place tonight.
   Past Participle A great banquet **has taken** place tonight.

8. The old man sits in the sun.
   Preterite The old man **sat** in the sun.
   Past Participle The old man **has sat** in the sun.

9. The Mexican swings the lasso round his head.
   Preterite The Mexican **swung** the lasso round his head.
   Past Participle The Mexican **has swung** the lasso round his head.

10. Johnson swims in the lake every day.
    Preterite Johnson **swam** in the lake every day.
    Past Participle Johnson **has swum** in the lake every day.

II.

Students were instructed to make two sentences containing each verb listed, one in the preterite (past) tense, one in the past participle (preceded by *have* or *has*). Answers will vary. The preterite and past participle form for each verb is shown below in bold print.

Set A

begin, **began, have begun**
drink, **drank, have drunk**
ring, **rang, have rung**
run, **ran, have run**
shrink, **shrank, have shrunk**
sing, **sang, have sung**
sink, **sank, have sunk**
spring, **sprang, have sprung**
swim, **swam, have swum**

Set B

bear, **bore, have borne**
bite, **bit, have bitten**
break, **broke, have broken**
choose, **chose, have chosen**
drive, **drove, have driven**
eat, **ate, have eaten**
fall, **fell, have fallen**
forget, **forgot, have forgotten**
freeze, **froze, have frozen**
hide, **hid, have hidden**
ride, **rode, have ridden**
shake, **shook, have shaken**
speak, **spoke, have spoken**
steal, **stole, have stolen**
swear, **swore, have sworn**
take, **took, have taken**
tear, **tore, have torn**
wear, **wore, have worn**

Chapter 105: Modifiers and Object of Infinitive or Participle

I.

Answers will vary. Suggestions are given.

1. I resolved to return **<u>quickly</u>** to England.
2. His orders to me were to keep him **<u>always</u>** in sight.
3. My first thought was to flee **<u>immediately</u>**.
4. To rush **<u>quickly</u>** towards her was my impulse.
5. What right have you, then, to upbraid me **<u>rudely</u>** for having told you the truth?
6. The young man began to spend his money **<u>lavishly</u>**.

II.

Students were instructed to circle the participles (which are shown in bold below), draw an arrow to the noun or pronoun each modifies (which is italicized and marked with an asterisks), and underline all the modifiers and objects of the participles. The first one was done for the student.

1. He occupied a *farm** of seventy acres, **situated** <u>on the skirts of that pretty little village</u>.
2. Mine was a small *chamber**, near the top of the house, **fronting** <u>on the sea</u>. *(William Black (1841-1898), Kilmeny)*
3. <u>The</u> **listening** *crowd** admire the lofty sound! *(John Dryden (1631-1700), "Alexander's Feast")*
4. This life, which seems so fair,
   Is like a *bubble** **blown** <u>up in the air</u>. *(William Drummond (1585-1649), "Madrigal LXXII")*
5. Still is <u>the</u> **toiling** *hand** of Care;
   The **panting** *herds** repose. *(Thomas Gray (1716-1771), "Spring")*
6. His bridge was only loose *planks** **laid** <u>upon large trestles</u>. *(Daniel Defoe (1660-1731), Memoirs of a Cavalier)*
7. She had a little room in the garret, where the maids heard *her** **walking** and **sobbing** <u>at night</u>. *(William Makepeace Thackeray (1811-1863), Vanity Fair)*
8. The kind *creature** retreated into the garden, **overcome** <u>with emotions</u>. *(William Makepeace Thackeray (1811-1863), Vanity Fair)*
9. The *colonel**, **strengthened** <u>with some troops of horse from Yorkshire</u>, comes up to the bridge. *(Daniel Defoe (1660-1731), Memoirs of a Cavalier)*
10. **Exhausted**, *I** lay down at the base of the pyramid. *(Thomas Moore (1779-1852), The Epicurean)*

Chapter 106: Principal Parts of Verbs

Students were instructed to complete the following tasks using the sentences from chapter 105, Exercise II (please refer to chapter 105 key for the sources of the sentences).

1. Underline all the subjects once and the present and past tense verbs twice.
2. Circle (shown in bold below) all the present and past participles and draw an arrow to the substantive which each modifies. (Shown in parentheses below.)
3. Label whether the verb is weak with W or strong with S in each case. (Shown next to the principle parts below.)
4. Write the principal parts of every verb on the lines provided.

1. He occupied a farm of seventy acres, **situated** (*farm*) on the skirts of that pretty little village.
   occupy, occupied, occupied (weak); situate, situated, situated (weak)

2. Mine was a small chamber, near the top of the house, **fronting** (*chamber*) on the sea.
   am, was, been (strong); front, fronted, fronted (weak)

3. The **listening** (*crowd*) crowd admire the lofty sound!
   listen, listened, listened (weak); admire, admired, admired (weak)

4. This life, which seems so fair,
   Is like a bubble **blown** (*bubble*) up in the air.
   seem, seemed, seemed (weak); am, was, been; blow, blew, blown (strong)

5. Still is the **toiling** hand of Care;
   The **panting** herds repose.
   am, was, been (strong); toil, toiled, toiled (weak); pant, panted, panted (weak); repose, reposed, reposed (weak)

6. His bridge was only loose planks **laid** (*planks*) upon large trestles.
   am, was, been (strong); lay, laid, laid (weak)

7. She had a little room in the garret, where the maids heard her **walking** (*her*) and **sobbing** (*her*) at night.
   have, had, had (weak); hear, heard, heard (weak); walk, walked, walked (weak); sob, sobbed, sobbed (weak)

8. The kind creature retreated into the garden, **overcome** (*creature*) with emotions.
   retreat, retreated, retreated (weak); overcome, overcame, overcame (strong)

9. The colonel, **strengthened** (*colonel*) with some troops of horse from Yorkshire, comes up to the bridge.
   strengthen, strengthened, strengthened (weak); come, came, came (strong)

10. **Exhausted** (*I*), I lay down at the base of the pyramid.
    exhaust, exhausted, exhausted (weak); lie, lay, lain (strong)

Chapter 107: Verbal Nouns Ending in -*ing* (Gerunds)

Students were instructed to underline all the words ending in -*ing* and label present participles with PP and verbal nouns with VN.

1. Books, **painting** (**VN**), **fiddling** (**VN**), and **shooting** (**VN**) were my amusements. *(Laurence Sterne (1713-1768), "Memoir of the Author" included in* The Life and Opinions of Tristam Shandy*)*

2. We are terribly afraid of Prince Eugene's **coming** (**VN**). *(Jonathan Swift (1667-1745), Letters)*

3. Upon **hearing** (**VN**) my name, the old gentleman stepped up. *(Oliver Goldsmith (1730-1774),* Vicar of Wakefield)

4. After I had resided at college seven years, my father died and left me — his **blessing** (**VN**). *(Oliver Goldsmith (1730-1774),* Citizen of the World)

5. The **neighing** (**VN**) of the generous horse was heard.

6. Joseph still continued a huge **clattering** (**VN**) with the poker. *(William Makepeace Thackeray (1811-1863),* Vanity Fair)

7. Then came the question of **paying** (**VN**).

8. The day had been spent by the king in sport and **feasting** (**VN**), and by the conspirators in **preparing** (**VN**)for their enterprise. *(Sir Walter Scott (1771-1832),* Tales of a Grandfather)

9. He first learned to write by **imitating** (**VN**) printed books. *(Samuel Johnson (1709-1784), "The Life of Alexander Pope")*

10. Here we had the pleasure of **breaking** (**VN**) our fast on the leg of an old hare, and some broiled crows. *(Thomas Gray (1716-1771), "Letters")*

Chapter 108: Future Tense

I.
Students were instructed to fill in the blanks with *will* or *shall*. Some of the sentences have hints to get the student started.

Futurity		*Promise or Determination*	
I shall	You will	I will	You shall
We shall	He/She/It will	We will	He/She/It shall
	They will		They shall

1. I am determined to learn my lesson. (*I will?* or *I shall?*) I **will** learn my lesson.

2. I am willing to accompany you. (*Will* or *shall?*) I **shall** accompany you.

3. You are sure to fall if you climb that tree. (*You will* or *you shall?*) You **will** fall if you climb that tree.

4. I am sure to fall if I climb that tree. (*I will* or *I shall?*) I **shall** fall if I climb that tree.

5. He is not to go home till he has learned his lesson. (*He will not* or *he shall not?*) He **shall** not go home till he has learned his lesson.

6. We agree to lend you fifty dollars. (*We will lend* or *we shall lend?*) We **will** lend you fifty dollars.

7. We are going to lend you fifty dollars, as a matter of fact. (*We will* or *we shall?*) We **shall** lend you fifty dollars, as a matter of fact.

8. We are determined to find the rascal who stole our dog. We **will** find the rascal who stole our dog.

9. We are certain to succeed in the search. We **shall** succeed in the search.

10. Columbus cannot fail to discover land if he sails on. Columbus **will** not fail to discover land if he sails on.

11. You are resolved to win this game, I see. You **shall** win this game, I see.

12. Are you willing to help me? (*Will you?* or *Shall you?*) **Will** you help me?

13. Are you to be punished? (*Will you?* or *Shall you?*) **Will** you be punished?

14. Are we to be punished? (*Will we?* or *Shall we?*) **Shall** we be punished?

II.
Students were instructed to fill in the blanks with *shall* or *will* as the sense requires. In some cases either may be used.

1. I __**shall**__ lose my train if I stay any longer.

2. I __**shall**__ be tired to death by night.

3. We __**shall**__ break through the ice if we are not careful.

4. We __**will**__ try to do our duty.

5. We __**will**__ not be guilty of such a crime.

6. We __**will**__ give you what you need.

7. I __**will/shall**__ send a letter to him at once, since you wish it.

8. "I __**shall**__ drown!" cried the poor fellow, who was struggling in the water. "Nobody __**will**__ help me!"

9. He __**will**__ misspell his words, in spite of all I can say.

10. They __will/shall__ not be captured if I can help it.

11. They __will__ catch nothing if they fish in that stream.

12. I __will__ catch one fish if I have to stay here all day.

13. I __shall__ catch cold in this carriage.

14. I __will__ ride as fast as I can.

Chapter 109: Passive Voice

I.
Students were instructed to complete the chart for each sentence. The answers are shown below.

1. The spears <u>are uplifted</u>; the matches <u>are lit</u>. *(Lord Byron (1788-1824), "The Siege of Corinth")*

Subject	**spears; matches**		
Verb phrase	**are uplifted; are lit**		
Verb tense	**present; present transitive, present; present transitive**		
Person	first	second	**<u>third</u>**
Number	singular	**<u>plural</u>**	

2. Burton <u>was staggered</u> by this news.

Subject	**Burton**		
Verb phrase	**was staggered**		
Verb tense	**past, transitive**		
Person	first	second	**<u>third</u>**
Number	**<u>singular</u>**	plural	

3. Thus <u>was</u> Corinth <u>lost</u> and <u>won</u>. *(Lord Byron (1788-1824), "The Siege of Corinth")*

Subject	**Corinth**		
Verb phrase	**was lost; (was) won**		
Verb tense	**past, transitive; past, transitive**		
Person	first	second	**<u>third</u>**
Number	**<u>singular</u>**	plural	

4. Five hundred carpenters <u>had been set</u> at work. *(Adapted from Jonathan Swift (1667-1745), Gulliver's Travels)*

Subject	**carpenters**		
Verb phrase	**had been set**		
Verb tense	**pluperfect, transitive**		
Person	first	second	**<u>third</u>**
Number	singular	**<u>plural</u>**	

5. Old Simon <u>is carried</u> to his cottage door. *(Thomas Hughes (1822-1896),* Tom Brown at Oxford*)*

Subject	**Old Simon** (students may simply write *Simon*)		
Verb phrase	**is carried**		
Verb tense	**present, transitive**		
Person	first	second	**<u>third</u>**
Number	**<u>singular</u>**	plural	

6. You <u>will be surprised</u> at her good spirits.

Subject	**You**		
Verb phrase	**will be surprised**		
Verb tense	**future, transitive**		
Person	first	**<u>second</u>**	third
Number	**<u>singular</u>**	plural	

7. George Brand <u>was ushered</u> into the little drawing room. *(William Black (1841-1898),* Sunset*)*

Subject	**George Brand**		
Verb phrase	**was ushered**		
Verb tense	**past, transitive**		
Person	first	second	**<u>third</u>**
Number	**<u>singular</u>**	plural	

8. We <u>shall be hit</u> by the sharpshooters.

Subject	**We**		
Verb phrase	**shall be hit**		
Verb tense	**future, transitive**		
Person	**<u>first</u>**	second	third
Number	singular	**<u>plural</u>**	

9. The house <u>had been struck</u> by lightning.

Subject	**house**		
Verb phrase	**had been struck**		
Verb tense	**pluperfect, transitive**		
Person	first	second	**<u>third</u>**
Number	**<u>singular</u>**	plural	

10. The art of writing <u>had</u> just <u>been introduced</u> into Arabia. *(Thomas Carlyle (1795-1881),* Heroes and Hero-Worship)

Subject	**art**		
Verb phrase	**had been introduced**		
Verb tense	**pluperfect, transitive**		
Person	first	second	<u>**third**</u>
Number	<u>**singular**</u>	plural	

11. They <u>are bred</u> up in the principles of honor and justice. *(Jonathan Swift (1667-1745),* Gulliver's Travels)

Subject	**They**		
Verb phrase	**are bred**		
Verb tense	**present, transitive**		
Person	first	second	<u>**third**</u>
Number	singular	<u>**plural**</u>	

12. He <u>was carried</u> away captive by the Indians.

Subject	**He**		
Verb phrase	**was carried**		
Verb tense	**past, transitive**		
Person	first	second	<u>**third**</u>
Number	<u>**singular**</u>	plural	

13. The alarm bell <u>will be rung</u> when the foe appears.

Subject	**bell**		
Verb phrase	**will be rung**		
Verb tense	**future, transitive**		
Person	first	second	<u>**third**</u>
Number	<u>**singular**</u>	plural	

14. For my own part, I swam as Fortune directed me, and <u>was pushed</u> forward by wind and tide. *(Jonathan Swift (1667-1745),* Gulliver's Travels)

Subject	**I**		
Verb phrase	**was pushed**		
Verb tense	**past, transitive**		
Person	<u>**first**</u>	second	third
Number	<u>**singular**</u>	plural	

15. Thus the emperor's great palace <u>was built</u>.

Subject	**palace**		
Verb phrase	**was built**		
Verb tense	**past, transitive**		
Person	first	second	**<u>third</u>**
Number	**<u>singular</u>**	plural	

16. The stranger <u>was surrounded</u>, <u>pinioned</u> with strong fetters, and <u>hurried</u> away to the prison of the great tower. *(William Beckford (1760-1844),* The History of Caliph Vathek)

Subject	**stranger**		
Verb phrase	**was surrounded, (was) pinioned, (was) hurried**		
Verb tense	**past, transitive**		
Person	first	second	**<u>third</u>**
Number	**<u>singular</u>**	plural	

17. Some of the cargo <u>had been damaged</u> by the sea water.

Subject	**cargo**		
Verb phrase	**had been damaged**		
Verb tense	**pluperfect, transitive**		
Person	first	second	**<u>third</u>**
Number	**<u>singular</u>**	plural	

18. Our blows <u>were dealt</u> at random.

Subject	**blows**		
Verb phrase	**were dealt**		
Verb tense	**past, transitive**		
Person	first	second	**<u>third</u>**
Number	singular	**<u>plural</u>**	

19. Nothing <u>will be gained</u> by hurry.

Subject	**Nothing**		
Verb phrase	**will be gained**		
Verb tense	**future, transitive**		
Person	first	second	**<u>third</u>**
Number	**<u>singular</u>**	plural	

20. I <u>shall be surprised</u> if he succeeds. *(Gouverneur Morris (1752-1816), "Diary and Letters")*

Subject	**I**		
Verb phrase	**shall be surprised**		
Verb tense	**future, transitive**		
Person	**<u>first</u>**	second	third
Number	**<u>singular</u>**	plural	

21. The orchards <u>were hewn</u> down. *(Lord Thomas Macaulay (1800-1859),* History of England*)*

Subject	**orchards**		
Verb phrase	**were hewn**		
Verb tense	**past, transitive**		
Person	first	second	**<u>third</u>**
Number	singular	**<u>plural</u>**	

22. Panama <u>was captured</u> by Morgan, the buccaneer.

Subject	**Panama**		
Verb phrase	**was captured**		
Verb tense	**past, transitive**		
Person	first	second	**<u>third</u>**
Number	**<u>singular</u>**	plural	

23. The bridge <u>will be swept</u> away by the flood.

Subject	**bridge**		
Verb phrase	**will be swept**		
Verb tense	**future, transitive**		
Person	first	second	**<u>third</u>**
Number	**<u>singular</u>**	plural	

24. My efforts <u>had been rewarded</u> with success.

Subject	**efforts**		
Verb phrase	**had been rewarded**		
Verb tense	**pluperfect, transitive**		
Person	first	second	**<u>third</u>**
Number	singular	**<u>plural</u>**	

25. The bank <u>was robbed</u> last night.

Subject	bank		
Verb phrase	**was robbed**		
Verb tense	**past, transitive**		
Person	first	second	<u>**third**</u>
Number	<u>**singular**</u>	plural	

II.

Answers will vary. Check to be sure that the passive voice is used. An example is shown for the first sentence.

1. delay <u>The game was delayed because of a lightning storm.</u>
2. devour
3. pierce
4. set
5. send
6. bring
7. betray
8. fulfill
9. declare
10. conduct
11. guide
12. spend
13. read
14. feel
15. catch
16. sink
17. cut
18. find
19. steal
20. drink
21. ring

Chapter 110: Active and Passive

I.

Students were instructed to change the active verbs to the passive voice without changing the meaning of the sentences.

1. Theseus killed the Minotaur. *The Minotaur was killed by Theseus.*

2. Fulton invented steamboats. *Steamboats were invented by Fulton.*

3. The President will veto the bill. *The bill will be vetoed by the President.*

4. Dampier explored the coast of Australia. *The coast of Australia was explored by Dampier.*

5. The Normans conquered the Saxons. *The Saxons were conquered by the Normans.*

6. A band of Indians attacked Deerfield. *Deerfield was attacked by a band of Indians.*

7. A storm has disabled the fleet. *The fleet has been disabled by the storm.*

8. The miner had found gold in the bed of the stream. *Gold had been found by the miner in the bed of the stream.*

9. John Greenleaf Whittier wrote "Snow-Bound." *"Snow-Bound" was written by J. G. Whittier.*

10. The sun will soon melt the snow. *The snow will soon be melted by the sun.*

11. Edison invented the incandescent electric light. *The incandescent electric light was invented by Edison.*

12. The Romans conquered Spain. *Spain was conquered by the Romans.*

13. The French settled Louisiana. *Louisiana was settled by the French.*

14. The Dutch colonized New York. *New York was colonized by the Dutch.*

15. Bruce defeated the English at Bannockburn. *The English were defeated by Bruce at Bannockburn.*

16. An English court declared Sir William Wallace guilty of treason. *Sir William Wallace was declared guilty of treason by an English court.*

17. Henry V defeated the French at Agincourt. *The French were defeated by Henry V at Agincourt.*

18. The Indians outwitted General Braddock. *General Braddock was outwitted by the Indians.*

19. Braddock had scorned Washington's advice. *Washington's advice had been scorned by Braddock.*

20. The Angles and Saxons invaded and subdued Britain. *Britain was invaded and subdued by the Angles and Saxons.*

II.

Analyze the sentences from chapter 109, Exercise I, reproduced below.

1. **Underline** complete subject **once** and complete predicate **twice**.
2. **Label** simple subject with **S** and simple predicate with **V**.
3. Place **parentheses** around phrases and brackets around clauses.
4. **Label** the parts of prepositional phrases with **Prep** for prepositions and **OP** for objects of the preposition.
5. **Label** any predicate adjectives with **PA** and predicate nominatives with **PN**.
6. **Label** any direct objects with **DO** and indirect objects with **IO**.
7. **Label** modifiers (adverbs **Adv**, adjectives **Adj**, adverb clauses **Adv**, adjective clauses **Adj**).

1. The (**Adj**) spears (**S**) (are uplifted) (**V**); the (**Adj**) matches (**S**) (are lit) (**V**). *(Lord Byron (1788-1824), "The Siege of Corinth")*

2. Burton (**S**) (was staggered) (**V**) (by (**Prep**) this (**Adj**) news (**OP**)) (**Adv phrase**).

3. Thus (**Adv**) was (**V**) Corinth (**S**) lost (**PA**) and (**C**) won (**PA**). *(Lord Byron (1788-1824), "The Siege of Corinth")*

4. (Five hundred) (**Adj**) carpenters (**S**) (had been set) (**V**) (at (**Prep**) work (**OP**)) (**Adv phrase**). *(Adapted from Jonathan Swift (1667-1745), Gulliver's Travels)*

5. Old (**Adj**) Simon (**S**) (is carried) (**V**) (to (**Prep**) his (**Adj**) cottage (**Adj**) door (**OP**)) (**Adv phrase**). *(Thomas Hughes (1822-1896), Tom Brown at Oxford)*

6. You (**S**) (will be surprised) (**V**) (at (**Prep**) her (**Adj**) good (**Adj**) spirits (**OP**))(**Adv phrase**).

7. George Brand (**S**) (was ushered) (**V**) (into (**Prep**) the (**Adj**) little (**Adj**) drawing (**Adj**) room (**OP**)) (**Adv phrase**). *(William Black (1841-1898), Sunset)*

8. We (**S**) (shall be hit) (**V**) (by (**Prep**) the (**Adj**) sharpshooters (**OP**)) (**Adv phrase**).

9. The (**Adj**) house (**S**) (had been struck) (**V**) (by (**Prep**) lightning (**OP**)) (**Adv Phrase**).

10. The (**Adj**) art (**S**) (of (**Prep**) writing (**OP**)) (**Adj phrase**) had (**V**) just (**Adv**) (been introduced) (**V**) (into (**Prep**) Arabia (**OP**)) (**Adv phrase**). *(Thomas Carlyle (1795-1881), Heroes and Hero-Worship)*

11. They (**S**) (are bred) (**V**) up (**Adv**) {in (**Prep**) the (**Adj**) principles (**OP**) (of (**Prep**) honor (**OP**) and (**C**) justice (**OP**)) (**Adj phrase modifying *principles*)}** (**Adv phrase modifying *are bred***). *(Jonathan Swift (1667-1745), Gulliver's Travels)*

12. He (**S**) (was carried) (**V**) away (**Adv**) captive (**Adv**) (by (**Prep**) the (**Adj**) Indians (**OP**)) (**Adv phrase**).

13. The (**Adj**) alarm (**Adj**) bell (**S**) (will be rung) (**V**) [when (**Adv**) the (**Adj**) foe (**S**) appears (**V**)] (**Adv clause**).

14. (For (**Prep**) my (**Adj**) own (**Adj**) part (**OP**)) (**Adj phrase**), I (**S**) swam (**V**) [as (**Adv**) Fortune (**S**) directed (**V**) me (**DO**),] (**Adv clause**) and (**C**) (was pushed) (**V**) forward (**Adv**) (by (**Prep**) wind (**OP**) and (**C**) tide(**OP**)) (**Adv phrase**). *(Jonathan Swift (1667-1745), Gulliver's Travels)*

15. Thus (**Adv**) the (**Adj**) emperor's (**Adj**) great (**Adj**) palace (**S**) (was built) (**V**).

16. The (**Adj**) stranger (**S**) (was surrounded) (**V**), pinioned (**V**) (with (**Prep**) strong (**Adj**) fetters (**OP**)) (**Adv phrase**), and (**C**) hurried (**V**) away (**Adv**) {(to (**Prep**) the (**Adj**) prison (**OP**) (of (**Prep**) the (**Adj**) great (**Adj**) tower (**OP**))} (**Adv phrase**). *(William Beckford (1760-1844), The History of Caliph Vathek)*

17. Some (**S**) (of (**Prep**) the (**Adj**) cargo (**OP**)) (**Adj phrase**) (had been damaged) (**V**) (by (**Prep**) the (**Adj**) sea (**Adj**) water (**OP**)) (**Adv phrase**).

18. Our (**Adj**) blows (**S**) (were dealt) (**V**) (at (**Prep**) random (**OP**)) (**Adv phrase**).

19. Nothing (**S**) (will be gained) (**V**) (by (**Prep**) hurry (**OP**)).

20. I (**S**) (shall be surprised) (**V**) [if (**C**) he (**S**) succeeds (**V**)] (**Subordinate conditional clause**). Conditional clauses are taught in Chapter 138.

21. The (**Adj**) orchards (**S**) (were hewn) (**V**) down (**Adv**). *(Gouverneur Morris (1752-1816), "Diary and Letters")*

22. Panama (**S**) (was captured) (**V**) (by (**Prep**) Morgan (**OP**), (the buccaneer) (**Appositive**)) (**Adv phrase**).

23. The (**Adj**) bridge (**S**) (will be swept) (**V**) away (**Adv**) (by (**Prep**) the (**Adj**) flood (**OP**)).

24. My (**Adj**) efforts (**S**) (had been rewarded) (**V**) (with (**Prep**) success (**OP**)) (**Adv phrase**).

25. The (**Adj**) bank (**S**) (was robbed) (**V**) (last (**Adj**) night) (**Adv**).

Do you notice a sentence pattern in a majority of these sentences? Describe the pattern here:
The majority of these sentences have this pattern:
Subject-passive voice verb phrase-adverb phrase or clause.

Chapter 111: Complete or Compound Tense

I.

In the following sentences underline all the verbs. Complete the chart for each sentence, identifying the subject, verb phrase, verb tense, person (circle the correct choice) and number (circle the correct choice).

1. My eldest daughter <u>had finished</u> her Latin lessons, and my son <u>had finished</u> his Greek. *(Robert Southey (1774-1843),* The Doctor*)*

Subject	**daughter**		
Verb phrase	**had finished**		
Verb tense	**pluperfect, active**		
Person	first	second	<u>**third**</u>
Number	<u>**singular**</u>	plural	

Subject	**son**		
Verb phrase	**had finished**		
Verb tense	**pluperfect, active**		
Person	first	second	<u>**third**</u>
Number	<u>**singular**</u>	plural	

2. There <u>has been</u> a heavy thunderstorm this afternoon.

Subject	**thunderstorm**		
Verb phrase	**has been**		
Verb tense	**perfect, passive**		
Person	first	second	<u>**third**</u>
Number	<u>**singular**</u>	plural	

3. A multitude of humming birds <u>had been attracted</u> thither. *(Nathaniel Hawthorne (1804-1864),* The House of Seven Gables*)*

Subject	**multitude**		
Verb phrase	**had been attracted**		
Verb tense	**pluperfect, passive**		
Person	first	second	<u>**third**</u>
Number	<u>**singular**</u>	plural	

4. Our men <u>had besieged</u> some fortified house near Oxford. *(Daniel Defoe (1660-1731),* Memoirs of a Cavalier*)*

Subject	**men**		
Verb phrase	**had besieged**		
Verb tense	**pluperfect, active**		
Person	first	second	**<u>third</u>**
Number	singular	**<u>plural</u>**	

5. I really <u>have had</u> enough of fighting.

Subject	**I**		
Verb phrase	**have had**		
Verb tense	**perfect, active**		
Person	**<u>first</u>**	second	third
Number	**<u>singular</u>**	plural	

6. All shyness and embarrassment <u>had vanished</u>. *(Susan Ferrier (1782-1854),* The Inheritance*)*

Subject	**shyness/embarrassment**		
Verb phrase	**had vanished**		
Verb tense	**pluperfect, active**		
Person	first	second	**<u>third</u>**
Number	singular	**<u>plural</u>**	

7. The great tree <u>has been undermined</u> by winter floods.

Subject	**tree**		
Verb phrase	**has been undermined**		
Verb tense	**perfect, passive**		
Person	first	second	**<u>third</u>**
Number	**<u>singular</u>**	plural	

8. He <u>had lost</u> his way in the pine woods.

Subject	**He**		
Verb phrase	**had lost**		
Verb tense	**pluperfect, active**		
Person	first	second	**<u>third</u>**
Number	**<u>singular</u>**	plural	

9. Thousands <u>had sunk</u> on the ground overpowered. *(Thomas Campbell (1777-1844), "The Soldier's Dream")*

Subject	**thousands**		
Verb phrase	**had sunk**		
Verb tense	**pluperfect, active**		
Person	first	second	<u>**third**</u>
Number	singular	<u>**plural**</u>	

10. A storm of mingled rain and snow <u>had come</u> on. *(William Godwin (1756-1836),* Travels of St. Leon*)*

Subject	**storm**		
Verb phrase	**had come**		
Verb tense	**pluperfect, active**		
Person	first	second	<u>**third**</u>
Number	<u>**singular**</u>	plural	

11. We <u>had left</u> our two servants behind us at Calais. *(Daniel Defoe (1660-1731),* Memoirs of a Cavalier*)*

Subject	**We**		
Verb phrase	**had left**		
Verb tense	**pluperfect, active**		
Person	<u>**first**</u>	second	third
Number	singular	<u>**plural**</u>	

12. The patience of Scotland <u>had found</u> an end at last. *(John Richard Green (1837-1883),* A Short History of the English People*)*

Subject	**patience**		
Verb phrase	**had found**		
Verb tense	**pluperfect, active**		
Person	first	second	<u>**third**</u>
Number	<u>**singular**</u>	plural	

13. His passion <u>has cast</u> a mist before his sense. *(John Dryden (1631-1700), "Palamon and Arcite," a poem retelling the "A Knight's Tale")*

Subject	**passion**		
Verb phrase	**has cast**		
Verb tense	**perfect, active**		
Person	first	second	<u>**third**</u>
Number	<u>**singular**</u>	plural	

14. The surgeon <u>has set</u> my arm very skillfully and well.

Subject	**surgeon**		
Verb phrase	**has set**		
Verb tense	**perfect, active**		
Person	first	second	<u>**third**</u>
Number	<u>**singular**</u>	plural	

15. A strange golden moonlight <u>had crept</u> up the skies. *(William Black (1841-1898), Kilmeny)*

Subject	**moonlight**		
Verb phrase	**had crept**		
Verb tense	**pluperfect, active**		
Person	first	second	<u>**third**</u>
Number	<u>**singular**</u>	plural	

16. You <u>will have finished</u> your task by Saturday.

Subject	**You**		
Verb phrase	**will have finished**		
Verb tense	**future perfect, active**		
Person	first	<u>**second**</u>	third
Number	<u>**singular**</u>	<u>**plural**</u>	

17. The wind <u>has howled</u> all day.

Subject	**wind**		
Verb phrase	**has howled**		
Verb tense	**perfect, active**		
Person	first	second	<u>**third**</u>
Number	<u>**singular**</u>	plural	

18. He <u>had gasped</u> out a few incoherent words. *(William Makepeace Thackeray (1811-1863), History of Pendennis)*

Subject	**He**		
Verb phrase	**had gasped**		
Verb tense	**pluperfect, active**		
Person	first	second	<u>**third**</u>
Number	<u>**singular**</u>	plural	

II.

Students were instructed to underline the infinitives and the participles and to parse them by writing the tense of each infinitive (present or perfect) and of each participle (present, past, or perfect).

1. Columbus's crew had begun <u>to despair</u>. **to despair: present infinitive**
2. I should like <u>to have seen</u> his face when he heard this news. **to have seen: perfect (see Section 472)**
3. I ought <u>to have known</u> that the lizard was harmless. **to have known: perfect (see Section 472)**
4. 'T is better <u>to have loved</u> and lost **to have loved: perfect (see Section 472)**
   Than never <u>to have loved</u> at all. **to have loved: perfect (see Section 472)**(*Alfred, Lord Tennyson (1809-1892), "In Memoriam"*)
5. <u>Having done</u> my best, I am ready <u>to endure</u> whatever comes. **Having done: perfect participle (see Section 471); to endure: present infinitive**
6. <u>Having</u> once <u>suffered</u> from the bite of a tarantula, Johnson was very much afraid even of harmless spiders. **Having suffered: perfect participle (see Section 471)**

Chapter 112: Progressive Verb Phrases, Part I

There are no written exercises for chapter 112.

Chapter 113: Progressive Verb Phrases, Part II

Students were instructed to double underline verbs and verb phrases and then parse them on the line, identifying the tense and whether or not it is progressive. The first one was done for them.

1. The church bells, with various tones, but all in harmony, <u>were calling</u> out and <u>responding</u> to one another. **were calling/were responding: past tense, progressive form** *(Nathaniel Hawthorne (1804-1864),* The House of Seven Gables)

2. A huge load of oak wood <u>was passing</u> through the gateway. **past tense, progressive form** *(Nathaniel Hawthorne (1804-1864),* The House of Seven Gables)

3. Many a chapel bell the hour <u>is telling</u>. **present, progressive** *(John Keats (1795-1821), "Isabella")*

4. Edmund <u>was standing</u> thoughtfully by the fire. **past, progressive** *(Jane Austen (1775-1817),* Mansfield Park)

5. A thick mist <u>was</u> gradually <u>spreading</u> over every object. **past, progressive** *(Susan Ferrier (1782-1854),* The Inheritance)

6. I <u>have been walking</u> by the river. **past perfect passive, progressive** *(Susan Ferrier (1782-1854),* The Inheritance)

7. Merry it <u>is</u> in the good greenwood **present, not progressive**

    When the mavis and merle <u>are singing</u>. **present, progressive**

    When the deer <u>sweeps</u> by, and the hounds <u>are</u> in cry, **sweeps: present, not progressive; are: present, not progressive**

    And the hunter's horn <u>is ringing</u>. **present, progressive** *(Sir Walter Scott (1771-1832), "Lady of the Lake")*

8. The morn <u>is laughing</u> in the sky. **present, progressive** *(Winthrop Mackworth Praed (1802-1839), "Gog")*

9. Curly-headed urchins <u>are gambolling</u> before the door. **present, progressive** *(Charles James Lever (1806-1872),* Harry Lorrequer)

Chapter 114: Emphatic Verb Phrases

Students were instructed to change the progressive and the emphatic forms to the ordinary tense forms. They were also to tell which of the "emphatic" forms are really emphatic.

1. The wind did blow, the cloak did fly. *(William Cowper (1731-1800), The Task)*
    The wind blew, the cloak flew.

2. Glossy bees at noon do fieldward pass. *(John Keats (1795-1821), "Isabella")*
    Glossy bees at noon fieldward pass.

3. A second time did Matthew stop. *(William Wordsworth (1770-1850), "Matthew")*
    Matthew stopped a second time.

4. He did come rather earlier than had been expected. *(Jane Austen (1775-1817), Mansfield Park)*
    He came rather earlier than was expected.

5. She did look a little hot and disconcerted for a few minutes. *(Susan Ferrier (1782-1854), The Inheritance)*
    She looked a little hot and disconcerted for a few minutes.

6. The dogs did bark, the children screamed,
    Up flew the windows all. *(William Cowper (1731-1800), "The Diverting History of John Gilpin")*
    The dogs barked, the children screamed,
    Up flew the windows all.

7. Our true friends do not always praise us.
    Our true friends always praise us not.

8. But Knowledge to their eyes her ample page,
    Rich with the spoils of time, did ne'er unroll. *(Thomas Gray (1716-1771), "Elegy Written in a Country Churchyard")*
    But Knowledge to their eyes her ample page,
    Rich with the spoils of time, ne'er unrolled. *"Ne'er unrolled" uses the emphatic to form a negative, but is not actually emphatic in meaning. See note on Section 482.*

9. Beasts did leap and birds did sing,
    Trees did grow and plants did spring. *(Richard Barnefield (1574-1620), "The Nightingale")*
    Beasts leapt and birds sang,
    Trees grew and plants sprang.

10. The noise of the wind and of the thunder did not awaken the king, for he was old and weary with his journey. *(Sir Walter Scott (1771-1832), Tales of a Grandfather)*
    The noise of the wind and of the thunder awakened not the king, for he was old and weary with the journey. *"Did not awaken" uses the emphatic to form a negative, but is not actually emphatic in meaning. See note on Section 482.*

11. Why did you not tell me the news?
    You told me not the news why? *This negative question does not have an emphatic meaning. See note on Section 482.*

12. I did tell you everything that I had heard.
    I told you everything that I heard.

13. Where does Mr. Jackson live? I do not know.
    Where lives Mr. Jackson? I know not. *"I do not know" uses the emphatic to form a negative, but is not actually emphatic in meaning. See note on Section 482.*

14. You did give me some anxiety by your long absence.
    You gave me some anxiety by your long absence.

15. Does this train go to Chicago?

     This train goes to Chicago? *This question is not emphatic in meaning. See note on Section 482.*

16. The conductor says that it does.

     The conductor says that it goes there. *This sentence has an ellipsis and the verb "go" is omitted.*

17. I did not believe that Jones was guilty of intentional falsehood; but I did think that he was rather careless in his account of what took place.

     I believed not that Jones was guilty of intentional falsehood; but I thought that he was rather careless in his account of what took place.

18. What did he tell you about Thomas?

     He told you what about Thomas? *This question is not emphatic in meaning. See note on Section 482.*

Chapter 115: Imperative Mood

Students were instructed to double underline the verb in each of the following sentences. Underline the subject once, when it is expressed; when not, supply it by writing it on the line provided.

1. (You) Let us have a walk through Kensington Gardens.
2. (You) Do not forget the poor.
3. (You) Hope not, base man, unquestioned hence to go! *(John Dryden (1631-1700), "Palamon and Arcite," a poem retelling the "A Knight's Tale")*
4. Would ye be blest? (You) Despise low joys, low gains. **Note: Students might have identified would ye *as a* verb, but this verb phrase is not imperative, but is a potential verb phrase (see chapter 128).** *(Alexander Pope (1688-1744), "Epistle to Mr. Murray")*
5. (You) Summon Colonel Atherton without a moment's delay.
6. (You) Look up and be not afraid, but hold forth thy hand. *(Sir Walter Scott (1771-1832), Quentin Durward)*
7. Mount ye! spur ye! (Ye) skirr the plain! *(Lord Byron (1788-1824), "The Siege of Corinth")*
8. (You) O, listen, listen, ladies gay! *(Sir Walter Scott (1771-1832), "Rosabelle")*
9. Toll ye the churchbell sad and slow. *(Alfred, Lord Tennyson (1809-1892), "The Death of the Old Year")*
10. You, Herbert and Luffness, alight,

    And bind the wounds of yonder knight. *(Sir Walter Scott (1771-1832), "Lady of the Lake")*
11. (You) Stay with us. (You) Go not to Wittenberg. *(William Shakespeare (1564-1616), Hamlet)*
12. (You) Listen to the rolling thunder.
13. (You) Call off your dogs!
14. (You) Keep thine elbow from my side, friend. *(Sir Walter Scott (1771-1832), Woodstock: Or, The Cavalier)*
15. (You) Do not leave me to perish in this wilderness.
16. (You) Saddle my horses! (You) Call my train together. *(William Shakespeare (1564-1616), King Lear)*

Chapter 115: Additional Review Exercise[1]

Students were instructed to **double underline** the verbs and verb phrases and **parse** them by telling all they can about the form and construction of each verb in the line provided. They should write the:

1. tense (or if it is an infinitive or participle, progressive or emphatic verb phrase)
2. voice (active or passive) and mood (indicative or imperative),
3. person (first, second, third)
4. number (singular or plural).

1. The more I <u>give</u> to thee, the more I <u>have</u>. **give: present , active indicative, first, singular; have: present , active indicative, first, singular** *(William Shakespeare (1564-1616),* Romeo and Juliet*)*

2. <u>Comes</u> the king back from Wales? **present, active indicative, third, singular** *(William Shakespeare (1564-1616),* King Henry IV Part Two*)*

3. <u>Dost</u> thou not <u>hear</u> them <u>call</u>? *dost hear:* **present, emphatic verb phrase, second, singular;** *call:* **infinitive with the subject** *them;* **the phrase** *them call* **is the direct object.** *(William Shakespeare (1564-1616),* King Henry IV Part One*)*

4. The more we <u>stay</u>, the stronger <u>grows</u> our foe. *stay:* **present, active indicative, first, plural;** *grows:* **present, active indicative, third, singular.** *(William Shakespeare (1564-1616),* King Henry VI Part Six*)*

5. I <u>know</u> not, gentlemen, what you <u>intend</u>. *know:* **present, active indicative, first, singular;** *intend:* **present, active indicative, second, singular/plural** *(William Shakespeare (1564-1616),* Julius Caesar*)*

6. How long <u>hast</u> thou <u>to serve</u>, Francis? *hast:* **present, active indicative, second, singular; to serve: infinitive** *(William Shakespeare (1564-1616),* King Henry IV Part One*)*

7. A great portion of my time <u>was passed</u> in a deep and mournful silence. **past, passive indicative, third, singular** *(William Godwin (1756-1836),* Travels of St. Leon*)*

8. The day, which <u>had been</u> tempestuous, <u>was succeeded</u> by a heavy and settled rain. *had been:* **pluperfect, active indicative, third, singular;** *was succeeded:* **past, passive indicative, third, singular**

9. His courage <u>was</u> not <u>staggered</u>, even for an instant. **past, passive indicative, third, singular** *(Sir Walter Scott (1771-1832),* Quentin Durward*)*

10. I <u>was startled</u> by the sound of trumpets. **past, passive indicative, first, singular** *(William Godwin (1756-1836),* Travels of St. Leon*)*

11. The company <u>was surprised</u> <u>to see</u> the old man so merry, when <u>suffering</u> such great losses; and the mandarin himself, <u>coming</u> out, <u>asked</u> him, how he, who <u>had grieved</u> so much, and <u>given</u> way to calamity the day before, <u>could</u> now <u>be</u> so cheerful? *(Oliver Goldsmith (1730-1774),* Citizen of the World*)*

was surprised: **past, passive indicative, third, singular;**

to see: **infinitive;**

suffering: **participle;**

coming: **participle;**

asked: **past, active indicative, third, singular**

had grieved: **pluperfect, passive indicative, third, singular;**

(had) given: **pluperfect, passive indicative, third, singular;**

could be: **infinitive, potential mood, third, singular--***Note: the student is not required to label this since it is not covered until chapter 128.*

(Continued on next page)

---

[1] Here chapters 90-115 should be reviewed.

"You <u>ask</u> me one question," <u>cries</u> the old man; "<u>Let</u> me <u>answer</u> by <u>asking</u> another: Which <u>is</u> the more durable, a hard thing or a soft thing; that which <u>resists</u> or that which <u>makes</u> no resistance?" (*Oliver Goldsmith (1730-1774), Citizen of the World*)

ask: **present, imperative, second, singular;**

cries: **present, indicative, third, singular;**

let: **present, imperative, second, singular;**

answer: **infinitive without *to*, used with the verb *let***

asking: **participle**

is: **present, indicative, third, singular;**

resists: **present, indicative, third, singular;**

makes: **present, indicative, third, singular.**

"A hard thing, <u>to be</u> sure," <u>replied</u> the Mandarin.
There you <u>are</u> wrong," <u>returned</u> Shingfu. "I <u>am</u> now four-score years old; and, if you <u>look</u> in my mouth, you <u>will find</u> that I <u>have lost</u> all my teeth, but not a bit of my tongue." (*Oliver Goldsmith (1730-1774)*, Citizen of the World)

to be: **infinitive**

replied: **past, active indicative, third, singular**

are: **present, active indicative, second, singular**

returned: **past, active indicative, third, singular**

am: **present, active indicative, first, singular**

look: **present, active indicative, second, singular**

will find: **future, active indicative, second, singular**

have lost: **perfect, active indicative, first, singular**

Chapter 116: Nominative Absolute

I.

Students were instructed to underline all nouns in the absolute construction and underline the participle in agreement. There were to mark above the participle whether each expresses the time with T, place with P, or circumstance of the action with C.

1. Navigation was at a stop, our <u>ships</u> neither <u>coming</u> (**C**) in nor <u>going</u> (**C**) out as before. *(Daniel Defoe (1660-1731), A Journal of the Plague Year)*

2. <u>Night</u> <u>coming</u> (**T**) on, we sought refuge from the gathering storm.

3. The <u>song</u> <u>ended</u>,(**T/C**) she hastily relinquished her seat to another lady. *(Susan Ferrier (1782-1854), The Inheritance)*

4. The house consisted of seven rooms, the <u>dairy</u> and <u>cellar</u> <u>included</u>. (**P**) *(Robert Southey (1774-1843), "A Yeoman's House in the Riding of Yorkshire")*

5. The <u>resolution</u> <u>being</u> thus <u>taken</u> (**C**), they set out the next day. *(Samuel Johnson (1709-1784), The History of Rasselas, Prince of Abyssinia: A Tale)*

6. They had some difficulty in passing the ferry at the riverside, the <u>ferryman</u> <u>being</u> (**C**) afraid of them. *(Daniel Defoe (1660-1731), A Journal of the Plague Year)*

7. She sat beneath the birchen tree,
Her <u>elbow</u> <u>resting</u> (**C**) on her knee. *(Sir Walter Scott (1771-1832), "Lady of the Lake")*

8. The <u>signal</u> of battle <u>being</u> <u>given</u> (**C/T**) with two cannon-shot, we marched in order of battalia down the hill. *(Daniel Defoe (1660-1731), Memoirs of a Cavalier)*

9. The dark lead-colored ocean lay stretched before them, its dreary <u>expanse</u> <u>concealed</u> (**C**) by lowering clouds. *(Susan Ferrier (1782-1854), The Inheritance)*

10. Next Anger rushed, his <u>eyes</u> [*being*] on fire. *Note: The participle is not expressed in this sentence. See Section 495. (William Collins (1721-1759), "An Ode for Music")*

11. The <u>last</u> of these voyages not <u>proving</u> (**C**) very fortunate, I grew weary of the sea. *(Jonathan Swift (1667-1745), Gulliver's Travels)*

12. The two Scottish <u>generals</u>, Macbeth and Banquo, <u>returning</u> (**C**) victorious from this great battle, their way lay over a blasted heath. *(Charles and Mary Lamb's Tales from Shakespeare, "Macbeth")*

13. The cottage was situated in a valley, the <u>hills</u> <u>being</u> (**C/P**) for the most part <u>crowned</u> (**C/P**) with rich and verdant foliage, their <u>sides</u> <u>covered</u> (**C/P**) with vineyards and corn, and a clear, transparent <u>rivulet</u> <u>murmuring</u> (**C/P**) along from east to west. *(William Godwin (1756-1836), Travels of St. Leon)*

14. <u>This</u> <u>done</u>, (**C**) the conspirators separated.

15. <u>This</u> <u>being</u> <u>understood</u>, (**C**) the next step is easily taken.

16. <u>This</u> <u>said</u>, (**C**) he picked up his pack and trudged on.

II.

Students were instructed to analyze the sentences in Exercise I, reproduced below. Refer to part I for the sources of the sentences.

Note: Some details are given below, such as the word that is modified by a particular phrase, for your clarification. Students were not asked to note the word modified.

1. <u>Navigation (**S**) was (**V**) (at (**Prep**) a (**Adj**) stop (**OP**)) (**Adv phrase**), [our (**Adj**) ships (**NA**) neither (**C**) coming (**NAP**) in (**Adv**) nor (**C**) going (**NAP**) out (**Adv**) (as (**Prep**) before (**OP**)) (**Adv phrase**)] (**NA Phrase**).</u>

2. <u>[Night (**NA**) coming (**NAP**) on (**Adv**)] (**NA phrase**), we (**S**) sought (**V**) refuge (**DO**) (from (**Prep**) the (**Adj**) gathering (**Adj**) storm (**OP**)) (**Adj phrase modifying** *refuge*).</u>

3. [The (**Adj**) song (**NA**) ended (**NAP**)] (**NA phrase**), she (**S**) hastily (**Adv**) relinquished (**V**) her (**Adj**) seat (**DO**) (to (**Prep**) another (**Adj**) lady (**OP**)) (**IO**).

4. The (**Adj**) house (**S**) consisted (**V**) (of (**Prep**) seven (**Adj**) rooms (**OP**)) (**PA phrase**), [the (**Adj**) dairy (**NA**) and (**C**) cellar (**NA**) included (**NAP**)] (**NA phrase**).

5. [The (**Adj**) resolution (**NA**) being (**NAP**) thus (**Adv**) taken (**NAP**)] (**NA phrase**), they (**S**) set (**V**) (out (**Adv**)) (the (**Adj**) next (**Adj**) day) (**Adverbial objective phrase--see Section 498;** *students have not yet studied the adverbial objective and do not need to identify this yet*).

6. They (**S**) had (**V**) some (**Adj**) difficulty (**DO**) (in (**Prep**) passing (**Verbal noun-OP**) the (**Adj**) ferry (**Obj of** *passing*) (at (**Prep**) the (**Adj**) riverside (**OP**)) (**Adj phrase**)), [the (**Adj**) ferryman (**NA**) being (**NAP**) afraid (**PA**) (of them) (**Adv phrase**)] (**NA phrase**).

7. She (**S**) sat (**V**) (beneath (**Prep**) the (**Adj**) birchen (**Adj**) tree (**OP**)) (**Adv phrase**),

   [Her (**Adj**) elbow (**NA**) resting (**NAP**) (on (**Prep**) her (**Adj**) knee (**OP**)) (**Adv phrase**)] (**NA phrase**).

8. [The (**Adj**) signal (**NA**) (of (**Prep**) battle (**OP**)) (**Adj phrase modifying** *signal*) (being given) (**NAP**) (with (**Prep**) two (**Adj**) cannon-shot (**OP**)) (**Adv phrase modifying** *being given*)] (**NA phrase**), we (**S**) marched (**V**) (in (**Prep**) order (**OP**)) (of (**Prep**) battalia (**OP**)) (down (**Prep**) the (**Adj**) hill (**OP**)).

9. The (**Adj**) dark (**Adj**) lead-colored (**Adj**) ocean (**S**) lay (**V**) stretched (**PA modifying** *ocean*) (before (**Prep**) them (**OP**)) (**Adv phrase modifying** *stretched*), [its (**Adj**) dreary (**Adj**) expanse (**NA**) concealed (**NAP**) (by (**Prep**) lowering (**Adj**) clouds (**OP**)) (**Adv phrase**)] (**NA phrase**).

10. Next (**Adv**) Anger (**S**) rushed (**V**), [his (**Adj**) eyes (**NA**) (on (**Prep**) fire (**OP**)) (**Adj phrase**)] (**NA phrase**).

11. [The (**Adj**) last (**NA**) (of (**Prep**) these (**Adj**) voyages (**OP**)) (**Adj phrase**) not (**Adv**) proving (**NAP**) very (**Adv**) fortunate (**Adj modifying** *last*)], (**NA phrase**) I (**S**) grew (**V**) weary (**PA**) (of (**Prep**) the (**Adj**) sea (**OP**))(**Adv phrase modifying** *weary*).

12. [The (**Adj**) two (**Adj**) Scottish (**Adj**) generals (**NA**), (Macbeth and (**C**) Banquo) (**Appositive**), returning (**NAP**) victorious (**Adj**) (from (**Prep**) this (**Adj**) great (**Adj**) battle (**OP**)) (**Adv phrase modifying** *returning*],(**NA phrase**) their (**Adj**) way (**S**) lay (**V**) (over (**Prep**) a (**Adj**) blasted (**Adj**) heath (**OP**)) (**PA phrase**).

13. The (**Adj**) cottage (**S**) (was situated) (**V**) (in (**Prep**) a (**Adj**) valley (**OP**)) (**Adv phrase**), [the (**Adj**) hills (**NA**) being (**NAP**) (for the most part) (**Adv phrase**) crowned (**NAP**) (with (**Prep**) rich (**Adj**) and (**C**) verdant (**Adj**) foliage (**OP**)) (**Adv phrase**), their (**Adj**) sides (**NA**) covered (**NAP**) (with vineyards and corn) (**Adv phrase**)], and [(**C**) a (**Adj**) clear (**Adj**), transparent (**Adj**) rivulet (**Adj**) murmuring (**NAP**) along (**Adv**) (from east) (**Adv phrase**) (to west) (**Adv phrase**)] (**3 NA phrases**).

14. [This (**NA**) done (**NAP**)] (**NA phrase**), the (**Adj**) conspirators (**S**) separated (**V**).

15. [This (**NA**) (being understood) (**NAP**)] (**NA phrase**), the (**Adj**) next (**Adj**) step (**S**) is (**V**) easily (**Adv**) taken (**V**).

16. [This (**NA**) said (**NAP**)], he (**S**) picked (**V**) up (**Adv**) his (**Adj**) pack (**DO**) and (**C**) trudged (**V**) on (**Adv**).

Chapter 117: Cognate Object and Adverbial Objective

Students were instructed to underline the cognate objects and the adverbial objectives, and parse each of them by writing on the line the noun class (common or proper), gender (M, F, or N), number (S, P), case, and whether it is a cognate object or adverbial objective.

1. But the skipper blew a **whiff** from his pipe,
   and a scornful **laugh** laughed he. *(Henry Wadsworth Longfellow (1807-1882), "The Wreck of Hesperus")*
   whiff: common noun, neuter, singular, objective, cognate object of the verb *blew*
   laugh: common noun, neuter, singular, objective, cognate object of the verb *laughed*

2. The wind blew a **gale**.
   gale: common noun, neuter, singular, objective, cognate object of the verb *blew*

3. Everybody looked **daggers** at the intruder.
   daggers: common noun, neuter, singular, objective, adverbial objective modifying *looked*

4. Speak the **speech**, I pray you, as I pronounce it to you. *(William Shakespeare (1564-1616), Hamlet)*
   speech: common noun, neuter, singular, objective, cognate object of the verb *speak*

5. The hail was terrific. The sky seemed to rain **stones**.
   stones: common noun, neuter, objective, cognate object of the verb *rain*

6. The colonists endured oppression a long **time**.
   time: common noun, neuter, objective, adverbial objective modifying *endured*

7. The poet Gray worked upon his "Elegy" several **years**.
   years: common noun, neuter, objective, adverbial objective modifying *worked*

8. That mountain is distant **five miles** from this spot.
   five miles: common noun phrase, neuter, objective, adverbial objective modifying *distant*

9. The soldiers marched **Indian file**.
   Indian file: proper noun phrase, neuter, objective, adverbial objective modifying *marched*

10. The table is **six feet** long, **four feet** wide, and **three feet** high.
    six feet: common noun phrase, neuter, objective, adverbial objective modifying *long*
    four feet: common noun, neuter, objective, adverbial objective modifying *wide*
    three feet: common noun, neuter, objective, adverbial objective modifying *high*

11. I cannot swim a **yard** farther.
    yard: common noun, neuter, objective, adverbial objective modifying *swim*

12. The cannon carried four **miles**.
    miles: common noun, neuter, objective, cognate object of verb *carried*

13. You will never accomplish anything **that way**.
    that way: common noun, neuter, objective, adverbial objective modifying *will accomplish*

14. The road ran a very long **distance** without a curve.
    distance: common noun, neuter, objective, cognate object of the verb *ran*

Chapter 118: Predicate Objective

I.
Students were instructed to fill in each blank with a predicate objective. Answers may vary. Suggestions are given.

1. The boys elected Will Sampson __**president**__ of the boat club.
2. I always thought your brother an excellent __**player**__ .
3. Do you call the man your __**friend**__ ?
4. The governor appointed Smith __**treasurer**__ .
5. Everybody voted the talkative fellow a __**nuisance**__ .
6. The pirates chose Judson __**captain**__ .
7. The hunter called the animal a __**threat**__ .
8. My parents named my brother __**John**__ .
9. I cannot think him such a __**fool**__ .
10. The merchant's losses made him a poor __**man**__ .
11. You called my brother a __**trickster**__ .

II.
Students were instructed to fill in each blank with a predicate adjective.

1. A good son makes his mother __**proud**__ .
2. The jury declares the prisoner __**guilty**__ .
3. This noise will surely drive me __**insane**__ .
4. I cannot pronounce you __**innocent**__ of this accusation.
5. The sedate burghers thought the gay youngster very __**silly**__ .
6. The travelers thought the river __**dangerous**__ .
7. Our elders often think our conduct __**foolish**__ .
8. I call the boy __**mature**__ for his age.
9. Exercise makes us __**fit**__ .
10. Nothing makes one so __**satisfied**__ as a good dinner.
11. Do you pronounce the prisoner __**innocent**__ ?
12. Do you think us __**rash**__ ?

III.
Students were instructed to analyze the sentences in I and II by completing the following steps.
1. **Identify** if the sentence is declarative, interrogative, imperative, or exclamatory by writing **D, Int, Imp,** or **Exc** in the blank on the left.
2. **Underline** the complete subject **once** and the complete predicate **twice**.
3. **Label** the simple subject with **S**, and the simple predicate with **V**.
4. **Label** the modifiers (**Adv, Adj**)
5. **Label** the direct object with **DO** and the transitive verb with **TV**, the predicate objective noun with **PO**, or predicate adjective used as predicate objective with **PO**.

Exercise I sentences:
1. D The (**Adj**) boys (**S**) elected (**TV**) (Will Sampson) (**DO**) president (**PO**) (of (**Prep**) the (**Adj**) boat (**Adj**) club (**OP**)) (**Adj phrase modifying** *president*).
2. D I (**S**) always (**Adv**) thought (**TV**) your (**Adj**) brother (**DO**) an (**Adj**) excellent (**Adj**) player (**PO**).
3. Int Do (**V**) you (**S**) call (**TV**) the (**Adj**) man (**DO**) your (**Adj**) friend (**PO**)?
4. D The (**Adj**) governor (**S**) appointed (**TV**) Smith (**DO**) treasurer (**PO**).

5. D   Everybody (**S**) voted (**TV**) the (**Adj**) talkative (**Adj**) fellow (**DO**) a (**Adj**) nuisance (**PO**).

6. D   The (**Adj**) pirates (**S**) chose (**TV**) Judson (**DO**) captain (**OP**).

7. D   The (**Adj**) hunter (**S**) called (**TV**) the (**Adj**) animal (**DO**) a (**Adj**) threat (**PO**).

8. D   My (**Adj**) parents (**S**) named (**TV**) my (**Adj**) brother (**DO**) John (**PO**).

9. D   I (**S**) can (**V**) not (**Adv**) think (**TV**) him (**DO**) such (**Adj**) a (**Adj**) fool (**PO**).

10. D   The (**Adj**) merchant's (**Adj**) losses (**S**) made (**TV**) him (**DO**) a (**Adj**) poor (**Adj**) man (**PO**).

11. D   You (**S**) called (**TV**) my (**Adj**) brother (**DO**) a (**Adj**) trickster (**PO**).

Exercise II sentences:

1. D   A (**Adj**) good (**Adj**) son (**S**) makes (**TV**) his (**Adj**) mother (**DO**) proud (**PO**).

2. D   The (**Adj**) jury (**S**) declares (**TV**) the (**Adj**) prisoner (**DO**) guilty (**PO**).

3. D   This (**Adj**) noise (**S**) will (**V**) surely (**Adv**) drive (**TV**) me (**DO**) insane (**PO**).

4. D   I (**S**) can (**V**) not (**Adv**) pronounce (**TV**) you (**DO**) innocent (**PO**) (of (**Prep**) this (**Adj**) accusation (**OP**)) (**Adv phrase modifying** *innocent*).

5. D   The (**Adj**) sedate (**Adj**) burghers (**S**) thought (**TV**) the (**Adj**) gay (**Adj**) youngster (**DO**) very (**Adv**) silly (**PO**).

6. D   The (**Adj**) travelers (**S**) thought (**TV**) the (**Adj**) river (**DO**) dangerous (**PO**).

7. D   Our (**Adj**) elders (**S**) often (**Adv**) think (**TV**) our (**Adj**) conduct (**DO**) foolish (**PO**).

8. D   I (**S**) call (**TV**) the (**Adj**) boy (**DO**) mature (**PO**) (for (**Prep**) his (**Adj**) age (**OP**)) (**Adv phrase modifying** *mature*).

9. D   Exercise (**S**) makes (**TV**) us (**DO**) fit (**PO**).

10. D   Nothing (**S**) makes (**TV**) one (**DO**) so (**Adv**) satisfied (**PO**) (as (**Prep**) a (**Adj**) good (**Adj**) dinner (**OP**)) (**Adv phrase**).

11. Int   Do (**V**) you (**S**) pronounce (**TV**) the (**Adj**) prisoner (**DO**) innocent (**PO**)?

12. Int   Do (**V**) you (**S**) think (**TV**) us (**DO**) rash (**PO**)?

IV.

Students were instructed to underline and label transitive verbs with TV, direct objects with DO, and predicate objectives with PO.

1. Pope **had** now **declared** (**TV**) **himself** (**DO**) a **poet** (**PO**). *(Samuel Johnson (1709-1784),* The Lives of Poets*)*

2. The people **call** (**TV**) **it** (**DO**) a backward **year** (**PO**). *(Thomas Gray (1716-1771), "Letter to His Mother")*

3. He **called** (**TV**) **them** (**DO**) untaught **knaves** (**PO**). *(William Shakespeare (1564-1616),* King Henry IV Part One*)*

4. He could **make** (**TV**) a small **town** (**DO**) a great **city** (**PO**). *(Francis Bacon (1561-1626), "Of Expense")*

5. She **called** (**TV**) **him** (**DO**) the best **child** (**PO**) in the world.

6. A man must be born a poet, but he may **make** (**TV**) **himself** (**DO**) an **orator** (**PO**). *(From the Latin adage, "Nascitur poeta, fit orator.")*

7. Fear of death **makes** (**TV**) many a **man** (**DO**) a **coward** (**PO**).

8. Ye **call** (**TV**) **me** (**DO**) **chief** (**PO**). *(Elijah Kellogg (1813-1901), "Ye Call Me Chief")*

9. The Poles always **elected** (**TV**) some **nobleman** (**DO**) their **king** (**PO**).

10. He cared not, indeed, that the world should **call** (**TV**) **him** (**DO**) a **miser** (**PO**); he cared not that the world should **call** (**TV**) **him** (**DO**) a **churl** (**PO**); he cared not that the world should **call** (**TV**) **him** (**DO**) **odd** (**PO**). *(Susan Ferrier (1782-1854),* The Inheritance*)*

V.

Students were instructed to change the verbs to passive voice.

What happens to the predicate objective or adjective? **The predicate objective or adjective becomes the direct object.**

Exercise II sentences:

1. A good son makes his mother proud. **A mother is made proud by her good son.**
2. The jury declares the prisoner guilty. **The prisoner is declared guilty by the jury.**
3. This noise will surely drive me insane. **I will be driven insane by the noise.**
4. I cannot pronounce you guilty of this accusation. **You cannot be pronounced guilty of this accusation.**
5. The sedate burghers thought the gay youngster very silly. **The gay youngster was thought very silly by the sedate burghers.**
6. The travelers thought the river dangerous. **The river was thought dangerous by the travelers.**
7. Our elders often think our conduct foolish. **Our conduct is often thought foolish by our elders.**
8. I call the boy mature for his age. **The boy is called mature for his age.**
9. Exercise makes us fit. **We are made fit by exercise.**
10. Nothing makes one so satisfied as a good dinner. **One is made satisfied by nothing as well as a good dinner.**
11. Do you pronounce the prisoner innocent? **Is the prisoner pronounced innocent by you?**
12. Do you think us rash? **Are we thought rash by you?**

Exercise IV sentences:

1. Pope had now declared himself a poet. **Pope was now declared a poet by himself.** *(Samuel Johnson (1709-1784), The Lives of Poets)*
2. The people call it a backward year. **It was called a backward year by the poet.** *(Thomas Gray (1716-1771), "Letter to His Mother")*
3. He called them untaught knaves. **They were called untaught knaves by him.** *(William Shakespeare (1564-1616), King Henry IV Part One)*
4. He could make a small town a great city. **A small town could be made a great city by him.** *(Francis Bacon (1561-1626), "Of Expense")*
5. She called him the best child in the world. **He was called by her the best child in the world.**
6. A man must be born a poet, but he may make himself an orator. **A man must be born a poet, but he by himself may be made an orator.** *(From the Latin adage, "Nascitur poeta, fit orator.")*
7. Fear of death makes many a man a coward. **Many a man are made a coward by the fear of death.**
8. Ye call me chief. **I am called chief by ye (thee *or* you).** *Note: "Ye" was used in the objective case, but typically the informal singular form was* thee *and is now* you. *(Elijah Kellogg (1813-1901), "Ye Call Me Chief")*
9. The Poles always elected some nobleman their king. **Some nobleman was always elected king by the Poles.**
10. He cared not, indeed, that the world should call him a miser; he cared not that the world should call him a churl; he cared not that the world should call him odd. **He cared not, indeed, that he was called a miser by the world; he cared not that he should be called a churl by the world; he cared not that he should be called odd by the world.** *(Susan Ferrier (1782-1854), The Inheritance)*

Chapter 119: Relative Pronouns

I.

In these exercises from chapter 51, Exercise III, students were instructed to circle (shown in bold below) all the relative pronouns and provide the following information:

(1) their number (**S, P**), person (**1st, 2nd, 3rd**), and gender (**M, F, M/F, N**);

(2) write their antecedents;

(3) identify their case (**N, G, O**).

1. A sharp rattle was heard on the window, **which** made the children jump. **which: S, 3rd, N, rattle, N**

2. The small torch **that** he held sent forth a radiance by **which** suddenly the whole surface of the desert was illuminated. **that: S, 3rd, N, torch, O; which: S, 3rd, N, radiance, O** *(Thomas Moore (1779-1852), The Epicurean)*

3. He **that** has most time has none to lose. **that: S, 3rd, M/F, He, N** *(Benjamin Disraeli (1804-1881))*

4. Gray rocks peeped from amidst the lichens and creeping plants **which** covered them as with a garment of many colors. **which: P, 3rd, N, lichens and plants, N** *(Susan Ferrier (1782-1854), The Inheritance)*

5. The enclosed fields, **which** were generally forty feet square, resembled so many beds of flowers. **which: P, 3rd, N, fields, N** *(Jonathan Swift (1667-1745), Gulliver's Travels)*

6. They **that** reverence too much old times are but a scorn to the new. **that: P, 3rd, M/F, They, N** *(Francis Bacon (1561-1626), "Of Innovations")*

7. The morning came **which** was to launch me into the world, and from **which** my whole succeeding life has, in many important points, taken its coloring. **which: S, 3rd, N, morning, N; which: S, 3rd, N, morning, O** *(Thomas De Quincey (1785-1859), Confessions of an English Opium-Eater)*

8. Ten guineas, added to about two **which** I had remaining from my pocket money, seemed to me sufficient for an indefinite length of time. **which: S, 3rd, N, two, O** *(Thomas De Quincey (1785-1859), Confessions of an English Opium-Eater)*

9. He is the freeman **whom** the truth makes free. **whom: S, 3rd, M, freeman, O** *(William Cowper (1731-1800), The Task)*

10. There was one philosopher **who** chose to live in a tub. **who: S, 3rd, M/F, philosopher, N** *(Robert Southey (1774-1843), The Doctor)*

11. Conquerors are a class of men with **whom**, for the most part, the world could well dispense. **whom: P, 3rd, M/F, class, O** *(Thomas Carlyle (1795-1881), Robert Burns)*

12. The light came from a lamp **that** burned brightly on the table. **that: S, 3rd, N, lamp, N**

13. The sluggish stream through **which** we moved yielded sullenly to the oar. **which: S, 3rd, N, stream, O** *(Thomas Moore (1779-1852), The Epicurean)*

14. The place from **which** the light proceeded was a small chapel. **which: S, 3rd, N, place, O**

15. The warriors went into battle clad in complete armor, **which** covered them from top to toe. **which: S, 3rd, N, armor, N** *(Sir Walter Scott (1771-1832), History of Scotland)*

16. She seemed as happy as a wave
    That dances on the sea. **that: S, 3rd, N, wave, N**
    (William Wordsworth (1770-1850), "The Two April Mornings")

17. He sang out a long, loud, and canorous peal of laughter, **that** might have wakened the Seven Sleepers. **that: S, 3rd, N, peal, N** *(Thomas De Quincey (1785-1859), Confessions of an English Opium-Eater)*

18. Thou hadst a voice **whose** sound was like the sea. **whose: S, 3rd, N, voice, G** *(William Wordsworth (1770-1850), "Sonnet to Milton")*

19. Many of Douglas's followers were slain in the battle in **which** he himself fell. **which: S, 3rd, N, battle, O** *(Sir Walter Scott (1771-1832), Tales of a Grandfather)*

II.

1. The **house** __which__ stands yonder belongs to Colonel Carton. *House* **is singular, 3rd person, neuter, as is** *which*.

2. Are you the **man** __who__ saved my daughter from drowning? *Who* **is singular, 3rd person, M, as is** *man*.

3. The sailor's wife gazed at the stately **ship** __which__ was taking her husband away from her. *Which* **is singular, 3rd person, N (could also be F), as is** *ship*.

4. A young **farmer**, __whose__ name was Judkins, was the first to enlist. *Whose* **is singular, 3rd person, M/F, as is** *farmer*.

5. **Nothing** __that__ you can do will help me. *That* **is singular, 3rd person, N, as is** *nothing*.

6. The **horses** __which__ belong to the squire are famous trotters. *Which* **is plural, 3rd person, N, as is** *which*.

7. James Adams is the strongest **man** __that__ I have ever seen. *That* **is singular, 3rd person, M/F, as is** *man*.

8. My **friend**, __whom__ we had overtaken on his way down town, greeted us cheerfully. *Whom* **is singular, 3rd person, M/F, as is** *friend*.

9. Behold the **man** __whom__ the king delighteth to honor! *Whom* **is singular, 3rd person, M, as is** *man*. *(Esther 6:9, adapted from King James Version)*

10. That is the **captain** __whose__ ship was wrecked last December. *Whose* **is singular, 3rd person, M/F, as is** *captain*.

III.

Students were instructed to make twelve sentences containing the pronouns given (some are listed twice). Answers may vary. Check to see that they used the relative pronouns appropriately.

1. who
2. whom
3. which
4. whose
5. of which
6. that
7. as
8. who
9. whom
10. which
11. whose
12. that

IV.

1. You find fault with *me,* who __am__ not to blame. **1st, S.** *Point out to your student that the verb must agree with the person and number, even though the antecedent in this example is in the objective case and the relative is nominative. In other words, in this example test the verb by saying, "I am..." See Section 509.*

2. *You* who ___are___ present are all members of the society. **2nd, P**

3. *We* who ___are___ in good health should have sympathy for the sick. **1st, P**

4. *He* who __is__ fond of good books will never feel lonely. **3rd, S**

5. *Those* of you who ___are___ ready may start at once. **3rd, P**

6. *I,* who ___am___ a poor swimmer, shall never win the prize. **1st, S**

7. *Nobody* who __is__ young ever really expects old age. **3rd, S**

8. Such of *us* as ___are___ aware of the facts have little doubt of the man's innocence. **1st, P**

Chapter 120: Gender of Relatives

There are no written exercises for chapter 120.

Chapter 121: Descriptive and Restrictive Relatives

Students were asked to identify each relative as descriptive or restrictive and be able to explain why in these sentences from Exercises II and III, chapter 51.

Exercise II sentences:

1. The house __which__ stands yonder belongs to Colonel Carton. *Restrictive*
2. Are you the man __who__ saved my daughter from drowning? *Restrictive*
3. The sailor's wife gazed at the stately ship __which__ was taking her husband away from her. *Restrictive*
4. A young farmer, __whose__ name was Judkins, was the first to enlist. *Descriptive*
5. Nothing __that__ you can do will help me. *Restrictive*
6. The horses __which__ belong to the squire are famous trotters. *Restrictive*
7. James Adams is the strongest man __that__ I have ever seen. *Restrictive*
8. My friend, __whom__ we had overtaken on his way down town, greeted us cheerfully. *Descriptive*
9. Behold the man __whom__ the king delighteth to honor! *Restrictive* (Esther 6:9, adapted from King James Version)
10. That is the captain __whose__ ship was wrecked last December. *Restrictive*

Exercise III sentences:

1. A sharp rattle was heard on the window, **which** made the children jump. *Descriptive*
2. The small torch **that** he held sent forth a radiance by which suddenly the whole surface of the desert was illuminated. *Restrictive* (Thomas Moore (1779-1852), The Epicurean)
3. He **that** has most time has none to lose. *Restrictive* (Benjamin Disraeli (1804-1881))
4. Gray rocks peeped from amidst the lichens and creeping plants **which** covered them as with a garment of many colors. *Restrictive* (Susan Ferrier (1782-1854), The Inheritance)
5. The enclosed fields, **which** were generally forty feet square, resembled so many beds of flowers. *Descriptive* (Jonathan Swift (1667-1745), Gulliver's Travels)
6. They **that** reverence too much old times are but a scorn to the new. *Restrictive* (Francis Bacon (1561-1626), "Of Innovations")
7. The morning came **which** was to launch me into the world, and from **which** my whole succeeding life has, in many important points, taken its coloring. *Restrictive, Restrictive* (Thomas De Quincey (1785-1859), Confessions of an English Opium-Eater)
8. Ten guineas, added to about two **which** I had remaining from my pocket money, seemed to me sufficient for an indefinite length of time. *Restrictive* (Thomas De Quincey (1785-1859), Confessions of an English Opium-Eater)
9. He is the freeman **whom** the truth makes free. *Restrictive* (William Cowper (1731-1800), The Task)
10. There was one philosopher **who** chose to live in a tub. *Restrictive* (Robert Southey (1774-1843), The Doctor)
11. Conquerors are a class of men with **whom**, for the most part, the world could well dispense. *Restrictive* (Thomas Carlyle (1795-1881), Robert Burns)

12. The light came from a lamp **that** burned brightly on the table. *Restrictive*

13. The sluggish stream through **which** we moved yielded sullenly to the oar. *Restrictive (Thomas Moore (1779-1852), The Epicurean)*

14. The place from **which** the light proceeded was a small chapel. *Restrictive*

15. The warriors went into battle clad in complete armor, **which** covered them from top to toe. *Descriptive (Sir Walter Scott (1771-1832), History of Scotland)*

16. She seemed as happy as a wave
    That dances on the sea. *Restrictive (William Wordsworth (1770-1850), "The Two April Mornings")*

17. He sang out a long, loud, and canorous peal of laughter, **that** might have wakened the Seven Sleepers. *Descriptive (Thomas De Quincey (1785-1859), Confessions of an English Opium-Eater)*

18. Thou hadst a voice **whose** sound was like the sea. *Restrictive (William Wordsworth (1770-1850), "Sonnet to Milton")*

19. Many of Douglas's followers were slain in the battle in **which** he himself fell. *Restrictive (Sir Walter Scott (1771-1832), Tales of a Grandfather)*

Chapter 122: The Relative Pronoun "What"

Students were instructed to change each *what* to *which* and explain.

1. We seldom imitate **what** we do not love.
   We seldom imitate **that which** we do not love.
   that = direct object of *imitate*; **which** = direct object of *do love*

   (Susan Ferrier (1782-1854), The Inheritance)

2. He gives us **what** our wants require.
   He gives us **that which** our wants require.
   that = direct object of *gives*; **which** = direct object of *our wants require*

3. **What**'s mine is yours, and **what** is yours is mine.
   That which is mine is yours, and **that which** is yours is mine.
   that = subject of *is mine*; **which** = subject of *is yours*;
   that = subject of *is yours*; **which** = subject of *is mine*

   (William Shakespeare (1564-1616), Measure for Measure)

4. **What** you have said may be true.
   That which you have said may be true.
   that = subject of *may be true*; **which** = direct object of *you have said*

5. **What** I have is at your service.
   That which I have is at your service.
   that = subject of *is at your service*; **which** = direct object of *I have*

6. The spendthrift has wasted **what** his father laid up.
   The spendthrift has wasted **that which** his father laid up.
   that = direct object of *The spendthrift has wasted*; **which** = direct object of *his father laid up*

7. **What** I earn supports the family.
   That which I earn supports the family.
   that = direct object of *I earn*; **which** = subject of *supports the family.*

8. **What** supports the family is Tom's wages.
   That which supports the family is Tom's wages.
   that = subject of is Tom's wages; **which** = subject of *supports the family*

Chapter 123: Compound Relative Pronouns

There are no written exercises for chapter 123.

Chapter 124: Relative Adjectives and Adverbs

I.
Students were instructed to underline the relatives and explain the construction of *that* and of *which*. Then change *that which* to *what* and explain the double construction of *what*.

1. <u>**That which**</u> man has done, man can do.

   that = direct object of *man can do*; **which** = direct object of *man has done*
   <u>**What** man has done, man can do.</u>
   What serves as the direct object of both clauses.
   (Marcus Garvey (1887-1940), "Speeches")

2. I will describe only <u>**that which**</u> I have seen.

   that = direct object of *I will describe*; **which** = direct object of *I have seen* **that** = predicate nominative of *Captivity is*; **which** = direct object of *I fear most*
   <u>I will describe only **what** I have seen.</u>
   What serves as the direct object of both clauses.

3. <u>**That which**</u> was left was sold for old iron.

   that = subject of *was sold*; **which** = subject of *was left*
   <u>**What** was left was sold for old iron.</u>
   What serves as the subject of both clauses.

4. <u>**That which**</u> inspired the inventor was the hope of final success.

   that = subject of *was the hope*; **which** = subject of *inspired the inventor*
   <u>**What** inspired the inventor was the hope of final success.</u>
   What serves as the subject of both clauses.

5. Captivity is <u>**that which**</u> I fear most.

   that = predicate nominative of *Captivity is*; **which** = direct object of *I fear most*
   <u>Captivity is **what** I fear most.</u>
   What serves as the predicate nominative of *Captivity is* and the direct object of *I fear most*.

6. <u>**That which**</u> we have, we prize not. <u>**That which**</u> we lack, we value.

   that = direct object of *we prize not*; **which** = direct object of *we have*;
   that = direct object of *we value*; **which** = direct object of *we lack*
   <u>**What** we have, we prize not. **What** we lack, we value.</u>
   What serves as the direct object of both clauses in both sentences.
   (Sentence adapted from William Shakespeare (1564-1616), Much Ado About Nothing)

7. I thought of <u>**that which**</u> the old sailor had told of storms and shipwrecks.

   that = object of preposition *of*, prepositional phrase *of that* is object of *thought*;
   which = direct object of *the old sailor had told*;
   <u>I thought of **what** the old sailor had told of storms and shipwrecks.</u>
   What serves as the object of *I thought* and the direct object of *the old sailor had told*.

8. Give careful heed to <u>**that which**</u> I say.

   that = object of preposition *to*, prepositional phrase *to that* is object of *heed*;
   which = direct object of *I say.*
   <u>Give careful heed to **what** I say.</u>
   What serves as the object of both clauses.

9. **That which** offended Bertram most was his cousin's sneer.
    that = subject of *was his cousin's sneer*; **which** = subject of *offended Bertram*.
    <u>**What** offended Bertram most was his cousin's sneer.</u>
    What serves as the subject of both clauses.

10. **That which** is done cannot be undone.
    that = subject of *cannot be undone*; **which** = subject of *is done*.
    <u>**What** is done cannot be undone.</u>
    What serves as the subject of both clauses.

Oral Exercise: Substitute *whatever* for *that which* whenever you can.

II.

Students were instructed to underline the relatives and explain their construction (*e.g.* direct object of subordinate clause).

1. <u>**Whoever**</u> he is, I will loose his bonds.
    Whoever is the subject of *he is* (think, "*whoever is he*"), the subordinate clause. Remember that *whoever* is the nominative case.

2. Give this message to <u>**whomever**</u> you see.
    Whomever is the object of the preposition *to* and with *to* it serves as the indirect object. **Whomever** has a double construction and also is the object of *you see*.

3. Give this letter to anyone <u>**whom**</u> you see.
    Whom is the object of *you see*. *Anyone* is the antecedent.

4. <u>**Whatsoever**</u> he doeth shall prosper.
    Whatsoever is the object of *he doeth* and the subject of *shall prosper*.

5. Everything <u>**that**</u> he does shall prosper.
    That is the object of *he does*. *Everything* is the antecedent.

6. I owe to you <u>**whatever**</u> success I have had.
    Whatever success is the object of *I owe* and *whatever* is the adjective modifying *success*.

7. I owe to you any success <u>**that**</u> I have had.
    That is the object of *I have had*. *Any success* is the antecedent.

8. <u>**Whoever**</u> deserts you, I will remain faithful.
    Whoever is the subject of *deserts you*.

9. He gave a full account of <u>**whatever**</u> he had seen.
    Whatever is the object of the preposition *of*, the object of *he had seen*.

10. <u>**Whichever**</u> road you take, you will find it rough and lonely.
    Whichever is an adjective modifying *road*.

Chapter 125: Interrogative Pronouns, Etc.

I.

Students were instructed to write fifteen interrogative sentences, using all the forms of the interrogative pronouns and adjectives. Answers will vary. Suggestions are given as a guide. Students may need to consult a dictionary for help with *whence* ("from what place or source") and *whither* ("to what place or state").

Interrogative pronouns
1. who: Who will write the letter?
2. which: Which of Shakespeare's plays is your favorite?
3. what: What character in *Much Ado About Nothing* do you like best?
4. whom: Whom shall I send?
5. whose: Whose book is on the table?

Interrogative adjectives
6. which: Which house is yours?
7. what: What color is it?

Interrogative adverbs
8. where: Where do you live?
9. when: When are you going to college?
10. whence: Whence did you come?
11. whither: Whither thou goest?
12. how: How do you make that dessert?
13. why: Why did you stay home?

Interrogative pronouns, adjectives, or adverbs of your choice
14. Answers will vary.
15. Answers will vary.

II.
Students were instructed to write the interrogative pronoun in the blank and circle its gender, number, part of speech, and case in the chart provided. Correct answers are shown in bold below.

1.   **Who** told you that I was going to London?

Interrogative pronoun	**Who**		
Gender	**masculine**	**feminine**	neuter
Number	**singular**	plural	
Part of speech	**substantive**	adjective	adverb
Case (if substantive)	**nominative**	objective	genitive
Noun modified (if adjective)			

2.   **What** is the meaning of this terrible summons? *(William Shakespeare (1564-1616),* Othello, The Moor of Venice*)*

Interrogative pronoun	**What**		
Gender	masculine	feminine	**neuter**
Number	**singular**	plural	
Part of speech	**substantive**	adjective	adverb
Case (if substantive)	**nominative**	objective	genitive
Noun modified (if adjective)			

3.   **Who** are these strange-looking men?

Interrogative pronoun	**Who**		
Gender	**masculine**	feminine	neuter
Number	singular	**plural**	
Part of speech	**substantive**	adjective	adverb
Case (if substantive)	**nominative**	objective	genitive
Noun modified (if adjective)			

4.   **What** dost thou want? **Whence** didst thou come?

Interrogative pronoun	**What**		
Gender	masculine	feminine	**neuter**
Number	**singular**	plural	
Part of speech	**substantive**	adjective	adverb
Case (if substantive)	nominative	**objective**	genitive
Noun modified (if adjective)			

Interrogative pronoun	**Whence**		
Gender	masculine	feminine	neuter
Number	singular	plural	
Part of speech	substantive	adjective	**adverb**
Case (if substantive)	nominative	objective	genitive
Noun modified (if adjective)			

5. **What** is the creature doing here?

Interrogative pronoun	**What**		
Gender	masculine	feminine	**neuter**
Number	**singular**	plural	
Part of speech	**substantive**	adjective	adverb
Case (if substantive)	nominative	**objective**	genitive
Noun modified (if adjective)			

6. **Which** of you is William Tell?

Interrogative pronoun	**Which**		
Gender	**masculine**	feminine	neuter
Number	**singular**	plural	
Part of speech	**substantive**	adjective	adverb
Case (if substantive)	**nominative**	objective	genitive
Noun modified (if adjective)			

7. **Where** did we go on that memorable night? **What** did we see? **What** did we do? Or rather, **what** did we not see, and **what** did we not do? *(Robert Southey (1774-1843),* The Doctor*)*

Interrogative pronoun	**Where**		
Gender	masculine	feminine	neuter
Number	singular	plural	
Part of speech	substantive	adjective	**adverb**
Case (if substantive)	nominative	objective	genitive
Noun modified (if adjective)			

Interrogative pronoun	**What (1)**		
Gender	masculine	feminine	**neuter**
Number	**singular**	plural	
Part of speech	**substantive**	adjective	adverb
Case (if substantive)	nominative	**objective**	genitive
Noun modified (if adjective)			

Interrogative pronoun	**What (2)**		
Gender	masculine	feminine	**neuter**
Number	**singular**	plural	
Part of speech	**substantive**	adjective	adverb
Case (if substantive)	nominative	**objective**	genitive
Noun modified (if adjective)			

Interrogative pronoun	**What (3)**		
Gender	masculine	feminine	**neuter**
Number	**singular**	plural	
Part of speech	**substantive**	adjective	adverb
Case (if substantive)	nominative	**objective**	genitive
Noun modified (if adjective)			

Interrogative pronoun	**What (4)**		
Gender	masculine	feminine	**neuter**
Number	**singular**	plural	
Part of speech	**substantive**	adjective	adverb
Case (if substantive)	nominative	**objective**	genitive
Noun modified (if adjective)			

8. Of **what** crime am I accused? **Where** are the witnesses?

Interrogative pronoun	**What**		
Gender	masculine	feminine	neuter
Number	singular	plural	
Part of speech	substantive	**adjective**	adverb
Case (if substantive)	nominative	objective	genitive
Noun modified (if adjective)	**crime**		

Interrogative pronoun	**Where**		
Gender	masculine	feminine	neuter
Number	singular	plural	
Part of speech	substantive	adjective	**adverb**
Case (if substantive)	nominative	objective	genitive
Noun modified (if adjective)			

9. **Whom** shall you invite to the wedding?

Interrogative pronoun	**Whom**		
Gender	**masculine**	**feminine**	neuter
Number	**singular**	**plural**	
Part of speech	**substantive**	adjective	adverb
Case (if substantive)	nominative	**objective**	genitive
Noun modified (if adjective)			

10. **Whose** are the gilded tents that crowd the way
    Where all was waste and silent yesterday? *(Thomas Moore (1779-1852),* Llalla Rookh)

Interrogative pronoun	**Whose**		
Gender	**masculine**	**feminine**	neuter
Number	singular	**plural**	
Part of speech	**substantive**	adjective	adverb
Case (if substantive)	nominative	objective	**genitive**
Noun modified (if adjective)			

Interrogative pronoun	**Where**		
Gender	masculine	feminine	neuter
Number	singular	plural	
Part of speech	substantive	adjective	**adverb**
Case (if substantive)	nominative	objective	genitive
Noun modified (if adjective)			

11. **Whom** did you see at my uncle's?

Interrogative pronoun	**Whom**		
Gender	**masculine**	**feminine**	neuter
Number	**singular**	**plural**	
Part of speech	**substantive**	adjective	adverb
Case (if substantive)	nominative	**objective**	genitive
Noun modified (if adjective)			

12. **What** strange uncertainty is in thy looks? *(Sir Walter Scott (1771-1832), Woodstock)*

Interrogative pronoun	**What**		
Gender	masculine	feminine	neuter
Number	singular	plural	
Part of speech	substantive	**adjective**	adverb
Case (if substantive)	nominative	objective	genitive
Noun modified (if adjective)	**uncertainty**		

13. **Which** of you trembles not that looks on me? *(William Shakespeare (1564-1616), Richard III)*

Interrogative pronoun	**Which**		
Gender	**masculine**	**feminine**	neuter
Number	**singular**	plural	
Part of speech	**substantive**	adjective	adverb
Case (if substantive)	**nominative**	objective	genitive
Noun modified (if adjective)			

14. To **whom** are you speaking?

Interrogative pronoun	**Whom**		
Gender	**masculine**	**feminine**	neuter
Number	**singular**	**plural**	
Part of speech	**substantive**	adjective	adverb
Case (if substantive)	nominative	**objective**	genitive
Noun modified (if adjective)			

15. From **whom** did you hear this news?

Interrogative pronoun	**Whom**		
Gender	**masculine**	**feminine**	neuter
Number	**singular**	**plural**	
Part of speech	**substantive**	adjective	adverb
Case (if substantive)	nominative	**objective**	genitive
Noun modified (if adjective)			

III.

Students were instructed to write ten exclamatory sentences beginning with *what*. Answers will vary. A suggestion is given to guide you. See Section 531.

1. What a great day for a walk in the park!

Chapter 126: The Infinitive as a Noun

I.

Students were instructed to replace each infinitive with a verbal noun ending in *-ing* and each noun ending in *-ing* with an infinitive.

1. To toil is the lot of mankind. <u>Toiling is the lot of mankind</u>.
2. To hunt was Roderick's chief delight. <u>Hunting was Roderick's chief delight</u>.
3. To aim and to hit the mark are not the same thing. <u>Aiming and hitting the mark are not the same thing</u>.
4. To swim is easy enough if one has confidence. <u>Swimming is easy enough if one has confidence</u>.
5. Wrestling is a favorite rural sport in the South of England. <u>To wrestle is a favorite rural sport in the South of England</u>.
6. To cross the river was Washington's next task. <u>Crossing the river was Washington's next task</u>.
7. To be poor is no disgrace. <u>Being poor is no disgrace</u>.
8. Begging was the poor creature's last resource. <u>To beg was the poor creature's last resource</u>.
9. Waiting for a train is tedious business. <u>To wait for a train is tedious business</u>.
10. To desert one's flag is disgraceful. <u>Deserting one's flag is disgraceful</u>.
11. Feeling fear is not being a coward. <u>To feel fear is not being a coward</u>.

II.

Students were instructed to analyze the sentences in I, as follows:
1. **Underline** the complete subject **once** and the complete predicate **twice**.
2. **Label** the simple subject with **S** and the simple predicate with **V**.
3. **Place** [brackets] around infinitives or verbal nouns and clauses and parentheses around phrases.
4. **Label** direct objects with **DO**, predicate nominatives with **PN**, and predicate adjectives with **PA**.
5. **Label** modifiers (**Adj**, **Adv**, etc.).

1. [To toil] (**S**) is (**V**) the (**Adj**) lot (**PN**) (of mankind) (**Adj phrase modifying *lot***).

2. [To hunt] (**S**) was (**V**) Roderick's (**Adj**) chief (**Adj**) delight (**PN**).

3. ([To aim] (**S**) and (**C**) [to hit] (**S**) (the mark) (**object of infinitive *to hit***)) (**S phrase**) are (**V**) not (**Adv**) the (**Adj**) same (**Adj**) thing (**PN**).

4. [To swim] (**S**) is (**V**) easy (**Adj**) enough (**Adv**) (if (**C**) one (**S**) has (**V**) confidence (**PN**)) (**subordinate conditional clause, *see chapter 138***).

5. [Wrestling] (**S**) is (**V**) a (**Adj**) favorite (**Adj**) rural (**Adj**) sport (**PN**) (in (**Prep**) the (**Adj**) South (**OP**) (of (**Prep**) England (**OP**)) (**Adj phrase**)) (**Adv phrase**).

6. [To cross] (**S**) the (**Adj**) river (**object of infinitive *to cross***) was (**V**) Washington's (**Adj**) next (**Adj**) task (**PN**).

7. [To be] (**S**) poor (**object of infinitive *to be***) (**S phrase**) is (**V**) no (**Adj**) disgrace (**PN**).

8. [Begging] (**S**) was (**V**) the (**Adj**) poor (**Adj**) creature's (**Adj**) last (**Adj**) resource (**PN**).

9. ([Waiting] (**S**) (for a train) (**Adv phrase modifying *waiting***)) (**S phrase**) is (**V**) tedious (**Adj**) business (**PN**).

10. ([To desert] (**S**) one's (**Adj**) flag (**object of infinitive *to desert***)) (**S phrase**) is (**V**) disgraceful (**PA**).

11. ([Feeling] (S) fear (**object of verbal noun *feeling***)) (**S phrase**) is (**V**) not (**Adv**) ([being] a (**Adj**) coward (**object of verbal noun *being***)) (**PN phrase**).

III.
Students were instructed to underline the infinitives and explain their construction (e.g. subject, object, etc.).

1. <u>To save</u> money is sometimes the hardest thing in the world. **Subject**

2. It is delightful <u>to hear</u> the sound of the sea. **Subject in sense.** *It* **is the grammatical subject, but is considered an** *expletive,* **or filler.** *To hear* **is technically considered in apposition to** *it.* **See Section 536 and the "Extra Resources: Miscellaneous Idioms," Section 7 at the end of this workbook.**

3. It was my wish <u>to join</u> the expedition. **Subject in sense, with the expletive** *it.* **See Section 536.**

4. Pity it was <u>to hear</u> the elfin's wail. **Subject in sense** *(Thomas Hood (1799-1845), "The Plea of the Midsummer Fairies")*

5. <u>To be</u> faint-hearted is indeed <u>to be</u> unfit for our trade. **To be (faint-hearted): Subject; To be (unfit...): Predicate Nominative** *(Daniel Defoe (1660-1731),* The Life of Colonel Jack)

6. Her pleasure was <u>to ride</u> the young colts and <u>to scour</u> the plains like Camilla. *(William Makepeace Thackeray (1811-1863),* Vanity Fair) *To ride* **and** *to scour:* **Predicate Nominative**

7. 'T is thine, O king, the afflicted <u>to redress</u>. **Subject** *(John Dryden (1631-1700), "Palamon and Arcite," a poem retelling the "A Knight's Tale")*

8. The queen's whole design is <u>to act</u> the part of mediator. **Predicate Nominative** *(Jonathan Swift (1667-1745), Letters)*

Chapter 127: The Infinitive as a Modifier

I.
Students were instructed to underline each infinitive and label the construction of each infinitive: as noun with **N**, as complementary infinitive (adverbial phrases modifying the verb) with **C**, as infinitive of purpose (adverbial phrases modifying the verb) with **P**, as adjective modifier of a noun with **Adj**, or as an adverbial modifier of the adjective with **Adv**.

1. All men strive <u>to excel</u>. **C, completing** *strive* *(Plutarch (45-120 AD), "Plutarch's Morals," translated by John Phillips)*
2. I have several times taken up my pen <u>to write</u> to you. **P, telling why he has taken up his pen.** *("Letter to Jonathan Swift from Mr. Addison, ")*
3. The moderate of the other party seem content <u>to have</u> a peace. **Adv, modifying** *content* *(Jonathan Swift (1667-1745), "Letter to Archbishop King")*
4. There was not a moment <u>to be</u> lost. **Adj modifying** *moment.* *(Lewis Carroll (1832-1898),* Alice's Adventures in Wonderland*)*
5. He chanced <u>to enter</u> my office one day. **C, completing** *chanced.*
6. The lawyer had no time <u>to spare</u>. **Adj modifying** *time.*
7. They tried hard <u>to destroy</u> the rats and mice. **C, completing** *tried*
8. This was very terrible <u>to see</u>. **Adv, modifing** *terrible.*
9. He continued <u>to advance</u> in spite of every obstacle. **C, completing** *continued.*
10. Even the birds refused <u>to sing</u> on that sullen day. **C, completing** *refused*
11. The bullets began <u>to whistle</u> past them. **C, completing** *began*
12. The fox was quick <u>to see</u> this chance to escape. **Adv, modifying** *quick*
13. That gaunt and dusty chamber in Granby Street seemed <u>to smell</u> of seaweed. **C, completing** *seemed (William Black (1841-1898), Kilmeny)*
14. Resolved <u>to win</u>, he meditates the way. **Adv, modifying** *resolved.* *(Alexander Pope (1688-1744), "Rape of the Lock")*
15. The explorer climbs a peak <u>to survey</u> the country before him. **P, telling why he climbed a peak**

II.
Students were instructed to make sentences with an infinitive following the verb, adjective, or participle. A sample is given for you. Answers will vary. Check to be sure that they have used infinitives properly.

VERBS:
1. begins: The day before the exam, he begins to study.

ADJECTIVES AND PARTICIPLES:
1. able: She is able to run an eight-minute mile.

Chapter 128: Potential Verb Phrases

I.
Students were instructed to double underline the potential verb phrases and parse the verb phrases by giving the:
1. tense
2. voice
3. person
4. number

1. She <u>might have held</u> back a little longer. *Permitted to have held; perfect, active, third person, singular*

2. The French officer <u>might</u> as well <u>have said</u> it all aloud. *Permitted to have said, perfect, active, third person, singular*

3. Is it possible that you <u>can have talked</u> so wildly? *Able to have talked, perfect, active, second person, singular*

4. An honest man <u>may take</u> a knave's advice. *Permitted to take, present, active, third person, singular*

5. If he <u>can</u>not <u>conquer</u> he may properly retreat. *Able to conquer, present, active, third person, singular*

6. I arrived at Oxford with a stock of erudition that <u>might have puzzled</u> a doctor, and a degree of ignorance of which a schoolboy <u>would have been</u> ashamed. *Permitted to have puzzled, perfect, active, third person, singular; Conditional consequence of something, perfect, passive, third person, singular*

7. From the hall door she <u>could look</u> down the park. *Was possibly able to look, past, active, third person, singular* (Jane Austen (1775-1817), Mansfield Park)

8. Early activity <u>may prevent</u> late and fruitless violence. *Is possible to prevent, present, active, third person, singular* (Edmund Burke (1729-1797), "Thoughts on the Cause of the Present Discontents")

9. Lear at first <u>could</u> not <u>believe</u> his eyes or ears. *Was possibly able to believe, past, active, third, singular* (Adapted from Charles and Mary Lamb's Tales from Shakespeare, "King Lear")

10. <u>May</u> I <u>come</u> back to tell you how I succeed? *Permit to come, present, active, first person, singular*

11. We <u>might have had</u> quieter neighbors. *Doubtful to have had, perfect, active, second person, plural*

12. It <u>must</u> then <u>have been</u> nearly midnight. *Necessarily have been, perfect, passive, third person, singular* (Thomas De Quincey (1785-1859), Confessions of an English Opium-Eater)

13. We <u>must have walked</u> at least a mile in this wood. *Necessarily have walked, perfect, active, second person, plural* (Jane Austen (1775-1817), Mansfield Park)

14. When bad men combine, the good <u>must associate</u>. *Obligated to associate, present, active, third person, plural* (Edmund Burke (1729-1797), "Thoughts on the Cause of the Present Discontents")

15. I <u>ought to be allowed</u> a reasonable freedom. *Moral obligation in past time, active, first person, singular* (Edmund Burke (1729-1797), "A Letter to a Noble Lord")

16. He <u>must</u> and shall <u>come</u> back. *Obligation to come, present, active, third person, singular*. Note: This sentence has a compound verb phrase. "He must...come" and "He...shall come," however only "must" indicates the meaning of obligation. "Shall" is an auxiliary verb that forms the future tense. (Jane Austen (1775-1817), Sense and Sensibility)

17. Something <u>must have happened</u> to Erne. *Necessarily have happened, perfect, third person, singular* (Henry Kingsley (1830-1876), The Hillyers and the Burtons: A Story of Two Families)

18. He <u>would</u> not <u>believe</u> this story, even if you <u>should prove</u> it by trustworthy witnesses. *Wish/consent to believe, past, active, third person, singular; Prove in the future, present, active, second person, singular.*

19. <u>Would</u> you <u>help</u> me if I <u>should ask</u> it? *Wish/consent to help, present, active, second person, singular; Ask in the future, present, active, first person, singular.*

20. <u>Should</u> you <u>care</u> if I were to fail? *Care in the future, present, active, second person, singular*

21. You <u>should obey</u> me if you were my son. *Duty or obligation to obey, present, active, second person, singular*

22. If he <u>should visit</u> Chicago, <u>would</u> he <u>call</u> on me? *Visit in the future, present, active, third person, singular; Willing to call, present, active, third, singular*

23. I <u>would go</u> if the others <u>would</u>. *Willing to go, present, active, first person, singular; Willing [to go], present, active, third person, plural*

II.

Students were instructed to analyze the sentences in I. Please refer to the answers to Exercise I for the sources of these sentences.

1. **Underline** the complete subject **once** and the complete predicate **twice**.
2. **Label** the simple subject with **S** and the simple predicate with **V**.
3. **Place [brackets]** around clauses and **(parentheses)** around phrases.
4. **Label** and identify the parts of phrases (**Prep** and **OP**, etc.).
5. **Label** direct objects with **DO**, predicate nominatives with **PN**, and predicate adjectives with **PA**.
6. **Label** modifiers (**Adj**, **Adv**, etc.), including phrases.

1. <u>She (**S**)</u> <u>(might have held) (**V phrase**) back (**Adv**) a little (**Adv**) longer (**Adv**)</u>.

2. <u>The (**Adj**) French (**Adj**) officer (**S**)</u> <u>might (**V**) (as well) (**Adv**) (have said) (**V**) it (**DO**) all (**Adj**) aloud (**Adv**)</u>.

3. <u>Is (**V**)</u> it <u>(**S**)</u> <u>possible (**PA**) (that (**C**) you (**S**) (can have talked) (**V phrase**) so (**Adv**) wildly (**Adv**)) (**Appositive clause in apposition with** *it*. **See** *Extra Resources: Miscellaneous Idioms* **at the end of** *Workbook* **2**)</u>?

4. <u>An (**Adj**) honest (**Adj**) man (**S**)</u> <u>(may take) (**V phrase**) a (**Adj**) knave's (**Adj**) advice (**DO**)</u>.

5. <u>(If (**C**) he (**S**) can (**V**) not (**Adv**) conquer (**V**)) (**Conditional subordinate clause**)</u> he <u>(**S**)</u> <u>may (**V**) properly (**Adv**) retreat (**V**)</u>.

6. <u>I (**S**)</u> <u>arrived (**V**) (at (**Prep**) Oxford (**OP**)) (**Adv phrase**) (with (**Prep**) [a stock (of (**Prep**) erudition (**OP** *of*))) (**OP** *with*) [that (**relative pronoun/S**) (might have puzzled) (**V phrase**) a (**Adj**) doctor (**DO**)] (**Adj clause modifying** *erudition*)], and (a degree (**OP** *with*) (of ignorance) (**Adj phrase modifying** *degree*) [of (**Prep**) which (**OP**) a (**Adj**) schoolboy (**S**) (would have been ashamed) (**V phrase**)] (**Adj clause modifying** *ignorance*))</u>.

7. <u>(From (**Prep**) the (**Adj**) hall (**Adj**) door (**OP**)) (**Adv phrase**)</u> she <u>(**S**)</u> <u>(could look) (**V phrase**) (down (**Prep**) the (**Adj**) park (**OP**)) (**Adv phrase**)</u>.

8. <u>Early (**Adj**) activity (**S**)</u> <u>(may prevent) (**V**) late (**Adj**) and (**C**) fruitless (**Adj**) violence (**DO**)</u>.

9. <u>Lear (**S**)</u> <u>(at (**Prep**) first (**OP**)) (**Adv**) could (**V**) not (**Adv**) believe (**V**) his (**Adj**) eyes (**DO**) or (**C**) ears (**DO**)</u>.

10. <u>May (**V**)</u> I <u>(**S**)</u> <u>come (**V**) back (**Adv**) [(to tell)(**infinitive complementary adverbial modifier of** *come*) you (**Obj of infinitive**) how (**Adv**) I (**S**) succeed (**V**)] (**Adv phrase modifying** *may come*)</u>?

11. <u>We (**S**)</u> <u>(might have had) (**V phrase**) quieter (**Adj**) neighbors (**DO**)</u>.

12. <u>It (**S**)</u> <u>must (**V**) then (have been) (**V phrase**) nearly (**Adv**) midnight (**Adv**)</u>.

13. <u>We (**S**)</u> <u>(must have walked) (**V phrase**) (at (**Prep**) least (**OP**)) (**Adj phrase modifying** *mile*) a (**Adj**) mile (**DO**) (in (**Prep**) this (**Adj**) wood (**OP**)) (**Adv phrase**)</u>.

14. <u>[When (**Adv**) bad (**Adj**) men (**S**) combine (**V**)] (**Adverbial clause**)</u>, the good <u>(**S**)</u> <u>(must associate) (**V phrase**)</u>.

15. <u>I (**S**)</u> <u>(ought to be allowed) (**V phrase**) a (**Adj**) reasonable (**Adj**) freedom (**DO**)</u>.

16. <u>He (**S**)</u> <u>must (**V**) and (**C**) (shall come) (**V phrase**) back (**Adv**)</u>.

17. <u>Something (**S**)</u> <u>(must have happened) (**V phrase**) (to (**Prep**) Erne(**OP**)) (**Adv phrase**)</u>.

18. <u>He (**S**)</u> <u>would (**V**) not (**Adv**) believe (**V**) this (**Adj**) story (**DO**), even (**Adv**) [if (**C**) you (**S**) (should prove) (**V phrase**) it (**DO**) (by (**Prep**) trustworthy (**Adj**) witnesses (**OP**)) (**Adv phrase modifying** *should prove*)] (**Adverbial conditional clause modifying** *believe*)</u>.

19. <u>Would (V) you (S) help (V) me (DO) [if (C) I (S) (should ask) (V **phrase**) it (DO)]</u> **(Adverbial conditional clause modifying** *help*)?

20. <u>Should (V) you (S) care (V) [if (C) I (S) were (V) (to fail)</u> **(infinitive as PN)]** **(Adverbial conditional clause modifying** *should care*)?

21. <u>You (S) (should obey) (V phrase) me (DO) [if (C) you (S) were (V) my (Adj) son (DO)]</u> **(Adverbial conditional clause modifying** *should obey*].

22. <u>[If (C) he (S) (should visit) (V phrase) Chicago (DO)]</u> **(Adverbial conditional clause modifying** *would call*), would (V) he (S) call (V) (on (Prep) me (OP))</u> **(Adverbial phrase modifying** *call*)?

23. <u>I (S) (would go) [if (C) the (Adj) others (S) (would [go]) (V phrase, *go* is omitted in ellipsis)]</u> **(Adverbial conditional clause modifying** *would go*). *Note: Students likely will not think of adding in the omitted verb "go," and ellipses are not covered in until chapter 143. Refer to this chapter as needed to explain this to your student.*

Chapter 129: Subjunctive Mood

Written exercises for subjective mood are given in chapter 132.

Chapter 130: Subjunctives in Wishes and Exhortations

Written exercises for subjective mood are given in chapter 132.

Chapter 131: Subjunctive in Concessions, Conditions, Etc.

Written exercises for subjective mood are given in chapter 132.

Chapter 132: Various Uses of the Subjunctive

I.

Students were instructed to complete a table of all the indicative and subjunctive forms of the verbs *be, have, do, bind, declare*, in the present and preterite active voice. Note that the archaic forms of *thou* are given for *to be, have*, and *do*, but most students will likely give the modern usage of the plural form "you" in the singular. This is perfectly acceptable.

To Be, *Active Voice*

INDICATIVE MOOD		SUBJUNCTIVE MOOD	
SINGULAR	PLURAL	SINGULAR	PLURAL
PRESENT TENSE			
1. *I am.* 2. *Thou art. (You are.)* 3. *He/she/it is.*	*We are.* *You are.* *They are.*	1. *If I be.* 2. *If thou be.* 3. *If he/she/it be.*	*If we be.* *If you be.* *If they be.*
PRETERITE TENSE			
1. *I was.* 2. *Thou wast/wert. (You were.)* 3. *He/she/it was.*	*We were.* *You were.* *They were.*	1. *If I were.* 2. *If thou wert. (If you were.)* 3. *If he/she/it were.*	*If we were.* *If you were.* *If they were.*

Have, *Active Voice*

INDICATIVE MOOD		SUBJUNCTIVE MOOD	
SINGULAR	PLURAL	SINGULAR	PLURAL
PRESENT TENSE			
1. *I have.* 2. *Thou hast. (You have.)* 3. *He/she/it has.*	*We have.* *You have.* *They have.*	1. *If I have.* 2. *If thou hast. (If you have.)* 3. *If he/she/it has.*	*If we have.* *If you have.* *If they have.*
PRETERITE TENSE			
1. *I had.* 2. *Thou hadst. (You had.)* 3. *He/she/it had.*	*We had.* *You had.* *They had.*	1. *If I* 2. *If thou hadst. (If you had.)* 3. *If he/she/it had.*	*If we had.* *If you had.* *If they had.*

Do, Active Voice

INDICATIVE MOOD		SUBJUNCTIVE MOOD	
SINGULAR	PLURAL	SINGULAR	PLURAL
PRESENT TENSE			
1. I do. 2. Thou doest. (You do.) 3. He/she/it does.	We do. You do. They do.	1. If I do. 2. If thou doest. (If you do.) 3. If he/she/it do.	If we do. If you do. If they do.
PRETERITE TENSE			
1. I did. 2. Thou didst. 3. He/she/it did. .	We did. You did. They did.	1. If I did. 2. If thou didst. (If you did.) 3. If he/she/it did.	If we did. If you did. If they did.

Bind, Active Voice

INDICATIVE MOOD		SUBJUNCTIVE MOOD	
SINGULAR	PLURAL	SINGULAR	PLURAL
PRESENT TENSE			
1. I bind. 2. You bind. 3. He/she/it binds.	We bind. You bind. They bind.	1. If I bind. 2. If you bind. 3. If he/she/it bind.	If we bind. If you bind. If they bind.
PRETERITE TENSE			
1. I bound. 2. You bound. 3. He/she/it bound.	We bound. You bound. They bound.	1. If I bound. 2. If you bound. 3. If he/she/it bound.	If we bound. If you bound. If they bound.

Declare, Active Voice

INDICATIVE MOOD		SUBJUNCTIVE MOOD	
SINGULAR	PLURAL	SINGULAR	PLURAL
PRESENT TENSE			
1. *I declare* 2. *You declare.* 3. *He/she/it declares.*	*We declare.* *You declare.* *They declare.*	1. *If I declare.* 2. *If you declare.* 3. *If he/she/it declare.*	*If we declare.* *If you declare.* *If they declare.*
PRETERITE TENSE			
1. *I declared.* 2. *You declared.* 3. *He/she/it declared.*	*We declared.* *You declared.* *They declared.*	1. *If I declared.* 2. *If you declared.* 3. *If he/she/it declared.*	*If we declared.* *If you declared.* *If they declared.*

Send, Passive Voice

INDICATIVE MOOD		SUBJUNCTIVE MOOD	
SINGULAR	PLURAL	SINGULAR	PLURAL
PRESENT TENSE			
1. *I am sent.* 2. *You are sent.* 3. *He/she/it is sent.*	*We are sent.* *You are sent.* *They are sent.*	1. *If I be sent.* 2. *If you be sent.* 3. *If he/she/it be sent.*	*If we be sent.* *If you be sent.* *If they be sent.*
PRETERITE TENSE			
1. *I was sent.* 2. *You were sent.* 3. *He/she/it was sent.*	*We were sent.* *You were sent.* *They were sent.*	1. *If I were sent.* 2. *If you were sent.* 3. *If he/she/it were sent.*	*If we were sent.* *If you were sent.* *If they were sent.*

Bind, Passive Voice

INDICATIVE MOOD		SUBJUNCTIVE MOOD	
SINGULAR	PLURAL	SINGULAR	PLURAL
PRESENT TENSE			
1. *I am bound.* 2. *You are bound.* 3. *He/she/it is bound.*	*We are bound.* *You are bound.* *They are bound.*	1. *If I be bound.* 2. *If you be bound.* 3. *If he/she/it be bound.*	*If we be bound.* *If you be bound.* *If they be bound.*
PRETERITE TENSE			
1. *I was bound.* 2. *You were bound.* 3. *He/she/it was bound.*	*We were bound.* *You were bound.* *They were bound.*	1. *If I were bound.* 2. *If were bound.* 3. *If he/she/it were bound.*	*If we were bound.* *If you were bound.* *If they were bound.*

Declare, Passive Voice

INDICATIVE MOOD		SUBJUNCTIVE MOOD	
SINGULAR	PLURAL	SINGULAR	PLURAL
PRESENT TENSE			
1. *I am declared.* 2. *You are declared.* 3. *He/she/it is declared.*	*We are declared.* *You are declared.* *They are declared.*	1. *If I be declared.* 2. *If you be declared.* 3. *If he/she/it be declared.*	*If we be declared.* *If you be declared.* *If they be declared.*
PRETERITE TENSE			
1. *I was declared.* 2. *You were declared.* 3. *He/she/it was declared.*	*We were declared.* *You were declared.* *They were declared.*	1. *If I were declared.* 2. *If you were declared.* 3. *If he/she/it were declared.*	*If we were declared.* *If you were declared.* *If they were declared.*

II.

Students were instructed to underline the subjunctive in each sentence, to explain the form (verb tense and voice), use (e.g. wish, exhortation, supposition, condition, etc.), meaning of each subjunctive, and write the section number from *Mother Tongue II* that applies to that sentence.

1. Mine <u>be</u> a cot beside the hill. **Present active, wish, see Section 561.** *(Samuel Rogers (1763-1855), "A Wish")*

2. Ruin <u>seize</u> thee, ruthless king! **Present active, wish, see Section 561.** *(Thomas Gray (1716-1771), "The Bard")*

3. It <u>were</u> madness to delay longer. **Past (preterite), what would have been, see Section 570.** *(Adapted from "Russell: or, The Rye-house Plot: a Tragedy in Five Acts")*

4. Of great riches there is no real use, except it <u>be</u> in the distribution. **Present, condition and doubt, see Section 564-565.** *(Francis Bacon (1561-1626), "Of Riches")*

5. King though he <u>be</u>, he may be weak. **Present, active, concession, see Section 563.** *(William Cowper (1731-1800), "Praise of Liberty")*

6. "God <u>bless</u> you, my dear boy!" Pendennis said to Arthur. **Present active, wish, see Section 561.** *(William Makepeace Thackeray (1811-1863),* History of Pendennis*)*

7. It is Jove's doing, and Jove <u>make</u> me thankful! **Present active, wish, see Section 561.** *(William Shakespeare (1564-1616),* Twelfth Night*)*

8. If this <u>were</u> played upon a stage now, I could condemn it as an improbable fiction. **Past (preterite) passive, supposed, Section 564-565.**

9. <u>Go</u> we, as well as haste will suffer us,

    To this unlooked for, unprepared pomp. **Present active, exhortation, see Section 562.** *(William Shakespeare (1564-1616),* King John*)*

10. If this <u>be</u> treason, make the most of it! **Present, condition and doubt, see Section 564-565.** *(Patrick Henry (1736-1799), "Give Me Liberty or Give Me Death")*

11. "Walk in." "I <u>had</u> rather <u>walk</u> here, I thank you." **Preterite active, idiomatic, see Section 571.** *(William Shakespeare (1564-1616),* Merry Wives of Windsor*)*

12. He looks as if he <u>were</u> afraid. **Preterite active, possibility, see Section 567.** *(Seeley Regester, nom de plume Metta Victoria Fuller Victor (1831-1885),* The Dead Letter*)*

13. I should have answered if I <u>had been</u> you. **Pluperfect, not a fact, see Section 564-565.**

14. God in thy good cause <u>make</u> thee prosperous! **Present active, wish, see Section 561.** *(William Shakespeare (1564-1616),* King Richard the Second*)*

15. These words hereafter thy tormentors <u>be</u>! **Present active, wish, see Section 561.** *(William Shakespeare (1564-1616),* King Richard the Second*)*

16. <u>Had</u> I a son, I would bequeath him a plough. **Preterite, condition, see Section 566.** *(Fanny Burney (1752-1840),* Cecilia: Or Memoirs of an Heiress*)*

17. There's matter in't indeed if he <u>be</u> angry. **Present, condition, see Section 564-565.** *(William Shakespeare (1564-1616),* Othello, The Moor of Venice*)*

18. I wish I <u>were</u> at Naples this moment. **Preterite, wish, see Section 561.**

19. If he <u>were</u> honest, he would pay his debts. **Preterite, condition, see Section 566.**

20. If wishes <u>were</u> horses, beggars might ride. **Preterite, is not a fact, see Section 565.** *(Nursery rhyme circa 16th century)*

21. No man cried, "God <u>save</u> him!" **Present, active, wish, see Section 561.** *(William Shakespeare (1564-1616),* King Richard the Second*)*

22. By heaven, methinks it <u>were</u> an easy leap

To pluck bright honor from the pale-faced moon. **Past (preterite), referring to future and expressing purpose, see Section 568 and 569. Compare** *Methinks [that] it were an easy leap...* *(William Shakespeare (1564-1616), King Henry IV Part One)*

23. Unless my study and my books <u>be</u> false,

    That argument you held was wrong in you. **Present, condition, see Section 564.** *(William Shakespeare (1564-1616), King Henry VI Part One)*

24. Take heed lest thou <u>fall</u>. **Present active, expressed purpose, see Section 568.** *(Adapted from I Corinthians 10:12)*

25. Though he <u>be</u> angry, he can do no harm. **Present, concession, see Section 563.**

Chapter 133: The Thought in the Sentence

There are no written exercises for chapter 133.

Chapter 134: Subordinate Clauses Classified

There are no written exercises for chapter 134.

Chapter 135: Clauses of Place and Time

Students were instructed to place brackets around each subordinate clause that was italicized for them and underline the relative pronoun or relative adverb.

I. ADJECTIVE CLAUSES

1. The town [*where John lives*] is called Granby.
2. The lion returned to the cave [*whence he had come*].
3. Show me the book [*in which you found the poem*].
4. There was no water in the desert [*through which he passed*].
5. The general fell at the moment [*when the enemy began to flee*].
6. Her father died on the day [*on which she was born*].

II. ADVERBIAL CLAUSES

1. The soldier died [*where he fell*].
2. He found his knife [*where he had left it*].
3. You make friends [*wherever you are*].
4. [*Whither thou goest*], I will go.
5. Washington lived [*when George III*] was king.
6. The poor fellow works [*whenever he can*].
7. We cannot start [*while the storm is raging*].
8. Jack rose from bed [*as the clock struck six*].
9. We reached our inn [*before the sun went down*].
10. Everybody waited [*until the speaker had finished*].
11. [*When the iron is hot*], then is the time to strike.

Chapter 136: Causal and Concessive Clauses

I.

Students were instructed to write ten sentences for each category: containing clauses of time, clauses of place, causal clauses, and concessive clauses. Review their sentences to be sure that they used the clauses properly.

II.

Students were instructed to use each of the following words to introduce a subordinate clause in a complex sentence and tell whether the clause that they have made expresses time, place, cause, or concession. Answers will vary, but check to be sure that they used the word in the clause and properly labeled it.

1. where
2. since
3. if
4. because
5. until
6. when
7. though

Chapter 137: Clauses of Purpose and Result

There are no written exercises for chapter 137.

Chapter 138: Conditional Sentences

There are no written exercises for chapter 138.

Chapter 139: Adverbial Clauses — Comparison

I.

Students were instructed to fill in the blanks below with *he* or *him* as the construction requires. The omitted verb is shown as an aid to explaining the reason for the choice.

You are older than ___**he [is]**___.

You can run faster than ___**he [can run]**___.

I am as strong as ___**he [is]**___.

We are as careful as ___**he [is]**___.

James is a better scholar than ___**he [is]**___.

II.

Students were instructed to place [brackets] around each subordinate clause. Tell whether the subordinate clauses express time, place, cause, concession, condition, purpose, result, or comparison.

1. [**As flattery was his trade**], he practiced it with the easiest address imaginable. **Condition** (*Oliver Goldsmith (1730-1774), Vicar of Wakefield*)

2. [**Whenever Macbeth threatened to do mischief to anyone**], he was sure to keep his word. **Time** (*Sir Walter Scott (1771-1832), Tales of a Grandfather*)

3. His armor was so good [**that he had no fear of arrows**]. **Result** (*Sir Walter Scott (1771-1832),* History of Scotland)

4. We admire his bravery, [**though it is shown in a bad cause**]. **Concession**

5. He talks [**as if he were a Spaniard**]. **Condition**

6. The marble bridge is the resort of everybody, [**where they hear music, eat iced fruits, and sup by moonlight**]. **Place** (*Thomas Gray (1716-1771), "Letter to His Father"*)

7. It was a fortnight after this, [**before the two brothers met again**]. **Result** (*Daniel Defoe (1660-1731),* A Journal of the Plague Year)

8. It was impossible for me to climb this stile, [**because every step was six feet high**]. **Cause** (*Jonathan Swift (1667-1745),* Gulliver's Travels)

9. The troops were hastily collected, [**that an assault might be made without delay**]. **Purpose**

10. Let us therefore stop [**while to stop is in our power**]. **Condition** (*Samuel Johnson (1709-1784),* The History of Rasselas, Prince of Abyssinia: A Tale)

11. King Robert was silent [**when he heard this story**]. **Result** (*Sir Walter Scott (1771-1832),* Tales of a Grandfather)

12. [**If others have blundered**], it is your place to put them to right. **Condition** (*Jane Austen (1775-1817),* Mansfield Park)

13. [**If Milton had any virtues**], they are not to be found in the Doctor's picture of him. **Condition** (*William Cowper (1731-1800), "Letter to Rev. William Unwin"*)

14. [**Where foams and flows the glorious Rhine**],

    Many a ruin wan and gray

O'erlooks the cornfield and the vine,

    Majestic in its dark decay.

Place (*Winthrop Mackworth Praed (1802-1839), "The Bridal of Belmont"*)

15. It was impossible for me to advance a step; [**for the stalks were so interwoven that I could not creep through**]. **Cause** (*Jonathan Swift (1667-1745)*, Gulliver's Travels)

16. [**If he is not here by Saturday**], I shall go after him. **Condition**

17. He laid his ear to the ground [that he might hear their steps]. **Purpose**

18. My passage by sea from Rotterdam to England was more painful to me [**than all the journeys I had ever made by land**]. **Comparison** (*Oliver Goldsmith (1730-1774)*, Citizen of the World)

19. Weeds were sure to grow quicker in his fields [**than anywhere else**]. **Comparison** (*Washington Irving (1783-1859), "The Legend of Sleepy Hollow"*)

Chapter 140: Direct and Indirect Statements

I.

Students were instructed to change the following statements to the form of indirect quotation after "He said that." Be sure to check that they have properly changed the verb form where necessary.

1. I found this diamond in South Africa. **He said that he found that diamond in South Africa.**

2. I shall sail for Yokohama next Tuesday. **He said that he will sail for Yokohama next Tuesday.**

3. My grandfather has given me a gold watch. **He said that his grandfather has given him a gold watch.**

4. I am not fond of poetry. **He said that he is not fond of poetry.**

5. I honor the memory of Mr. Gladstone. **He said that he honors the memory of Mr. Gladstone.**

6. Lieutenant Peary has just returned from the Arctic regions. **He said that Lieutenant Peary has just returned from the Arctic regions.**

7. You will certainly visit the pyramids. **He said that you will certainly visit the pyramids.**

8. John is stronger than Thomas. **He said that John is stronger than Thomas.**

9. This bird's wing has been broken. **He said that this bird's wing has been broken.**

10. The trapper is struggling with a huge bear. **He said that the trapper is struggling with a huge bear.**

11. My home is on the prairie. **He said that his home is on the prairie.**

12. Louisiana formerly belonged to France. **He said that Louisiana formerly belonged to France.**

II.

Students were instructed to turn each sentence from Exercise I into a direct quotation using quotation marks and the prefix "He said," and compare the results with the original sentences. Be sure to punctuate properly.

1. I found this diamond in South Africa. **He said, "I found this diamond in South Africa."**

2. I shall sail for Yokohama next Tuesday. **He said, "I shall sail for Yokohama next Tuesday."**

3. My grandfather has given me a gold watch. **He said, "My grandfather has given me a gold watch."**

4. I am not fond of poetry. **He said, "I am not fond of poetry."**

5. I honor the memory of Mr. Gladstone. **He said, "I honor the memory of Mr. Gladstone."**

6. Lieutenant Peary has just returned from the Arctic regions. **He said, "Lieutenant Peary has just returned from the Arctic regions."**

7. You will certainly visit the pyramids. **He said, "You will certainly visit the pyramids."**

8. John is stronger than Thomas. **He said, "John is stronger than Thomas."**

9. This bird's wing has been broken. **He said, "This bird's wing has been broken."**

10. The trapper is struggling with a huge bear. **He said, "The trapper is struggling with a huge bear."**

11. My home is on the prairie. **He said, "My home is on the prairie."**

12. Louisiana formerly belonged to France. **He said, "Louisiana formerly belonged to France."**

Chapter 141: Indirect Questions

Students were instructed to place brackets around the substantive clauses. Label the construction of each (as subject with S, object with O, etc.), and write in the blank on the left whether it is an indirect statement (S) or an indirect question (Q).

1. <u>Sub, S</u> [That fine feathers do not make fine birds] has always been taught by philosophers. *(This classic proverb appears in George Washington's advice to his nephew in 1783.)*

2. <u>Obj, Q</u> Here we halted in the open field, and sent out our people to see [how things were in the country]. *(Daniel Defoe (1660-1731), Memoirs of a Cavalier)*

3. <u>Obj, S</u> I do not imagine [that you find me rash in declaring myself]. *(Edmund Burke (1729-1797), "Speech at the Conclusion of a Poll")*

4. <u>Obj, Q</u> [What became of my companions] I cannot tell. *(Jonathan Swift (1667-1745), Gulliver's Travels)*

5. <u>Obj, S</u> I should now tell [what public measures were taken by the magistrates for the general safety]. *(Daniel Defoe (1660-1731), A Journal of the Plague Year)*

6. <u>Obj, S</u> You see, my lord, [how things are altered]. *(Jonathan Swift (1667-1745), "Letter to Archbishop King")*

7. <u>PN, Q</u> Now the question was, [what I should do next].

8. <u>Obj, S</u> He said [that he was going over to Greenwich]. *(Daniel Defoe (1660-1731), A Journal of the Plague Year)*

    <u>Obj, Q</u> I asked [if he would let me go with him].

9. <u>Sub, S</u> [That the tide is rising] may be seen by anybody.

10. <u>Obj, S</u> Ask me no reason [why I love you].

11. <u>Sub, S</u> [That Arnold was a traitor] was now clear enough.

12. <u>Obj, S</u> I doubt [whether this act is legal].

13. <u>Obj, S</u> I am not prepared to say [that Knox had a soft temper];

    <u>Obj, S</u> nor do I know [that he had an ill temper]. *(Thomas Carlyle (1795-1881), "Lectures on Heroes")*

14. <u>PN, Q</u> There are two questions, — [whether the Essay will succeed],

    <u>PN, Q</u> and [who or what is the author]. *(Samuel Johnson (1709-1784), "The Life of Alexander Pope")*

15. <u>Obj, S</u> The shouts of storm and successful violence announced [that the castle was in the act of being taken]. *(Sir Walter Scott (1771-1832), Quentin Durward)*

16. <u>Obj, Q</u> The stranger inquired [where the mayor lived].

17. <u>Sub, S</u> [That all is not gold that glitters] was found out long ago.

18. <u>Obj, Q</u> I demanded [why the gates were shut].

19. <u>Obj, S</u> I doubt [if I ever talked so much nonsense in my life].

20. <u>Obj, S</u> I solemnly assure you [that you are quite mistaken].

21. <u>Obj, S</u> The prince soon concluded [that he should never be happy in this course of life]. *Samuel Johnson (1709-1784), The History of Rasselas, Prince of Abyssinia: A Tale)*

22. <u>Obj, Q</u> I know not [what others may think].

23. <u>Obj, S</u> Tell me not [that life is a dream].

24. <u>Obj, S</u> I think [you are mistaken].

Chapter 142: Infinitive Clauses

Students were instructed to make ten sentences containing infinitive clauses after verbs of *wishing, commanding, believing, declaring,* etc. Consider these examples:

My father wishes me to become a lawyer. (Verb of *wishing*)
She wants him to read five books. (Verb of *wishing*)
Joanna told her to sing a song. (Verb of *commanding*)
Sydney believes him to be capable. (Verb of *believing*)
Hope declares him to be the winner. (Verb of *declaring*)

Answers will vary. Look to see that the sentences follow these patterns and refer to Chapter 142 to be sure that the student understands.

Chapter 143: Elliptical Sentences

Students were instructed to rewrite and supply the ellipsis in each of the following elliptical sentences. Examples in chapter 143 are helpful.

1. When in need of help, apply to me. **When <u>you are</u> in need of help, apply to me.**
2. The leader they chose was called Pedro. **The leader <u>that</u> they chose was called Pedro.**
3. A good conscience is better than gold. **A good conscience is better than gold <u>is</u>.**
4. You are much taller than I. **You are much taller than I <u>am</u>.**
5. Tom likes you better than me. **Tom likes you better than <u>he likes</u> me.**
6. Though beaten, I am not discouraged. **Though <u>I am</u> beaten, I am not discouraged.**
7. I will send you the money tomorrow, if possible. **I will send you the month tomorrow, if <u>it is</u> possible.**
8. Why all this noise? **Why <u>is there</u> all this noise?**
9. Some of us are studying arithmetic, others algebra. **Some of us are studying arithmetic, others <u>are studying</u> algebra.**
10. The book you were reading has been returned to the library. **The book <u>that</u> you were reading has been returned to the library.**
11. I don't believe you know your lesson. **I don't believe <u>that</u> you know your lesson.**
12. What next? **What <u>is</u> next?**
13. When inclined to lose your temper, count twenty before you speak. **When <u>you are</u> inclined to lose your temper, <u>you should</u> count <u>to</u> twenty before you speak.**
14. "Whither bound?" asked the captain. **"Whither <u>are you</u> bound?" asked the captain.**
15. Beetles have six legs, spiders eight. **Beetles have six legs, spiders <u>have</u> eight.**
16. Your boat is painted white, George's green. **Your boat is painted white, George's <u>boat is painted</u> green.**
17. I bought this hat at Sampson's. **I bought this hat at Sampson's <u>store.</u>**
18. These apples, though handsome enough, are rather hard. **These apples, though <u>they are</u> handsome enough, are rather hard.**

Punctuation Practice: Exercise A

The proper capitalization and punctuation is shown.

1. Is it your will, brethren, that this man be elected to the council?
2. Hark! How the pitiless tempest raves!
3. Tom, however, was not pleased with the prospect.
4. Nothing, I trust, will interfere with your plan.
5. The fisherman wades in the surges,
   The sailor sails over the sea,
   The soldier steps bravely to battle,
   The woodman lays axe to the tree.
6. Neither witch nor warlock crossed Mordaunt's path, however. *(Sir Walter Scott (1771-1832), The Pirate)*

Punctuation Practice: Exercise B

The proper capitalization and punctuation is shown.

1. The horse was injured in one of his hind legs.
2. Esther was going to see if she could get some fresh eggs for her mistress's breakfast before the shops closed.
3. All speech, even the commonest speech, has something of song in it.
4. Sam ran out to hold his father's horse.
5. "Now doctor," cried the boys, "do tell us your adventures!" *(Henry Kingsley (1830-1876), The Recollections of Geoffrey Hamlyn)*
6. Our English archers bent their bows,
   Their hearts were good and true;
   At the first flight of arrows sent,
   Full fourscore scots they slew.
   ("Ballad of Chevy-Chase")
7. The bridegroom stood dangling his bonnet and plume. *(Sir Walter Scott (1771-1832), "Marmion")*
8. Emma was sitting in the midst of the children, telling them a story; and she came smiling towards Erne, holding out her hand. *(Henry Kingsley (1830-1876), The Hillyers and the Burtons: A Story of Two Families)*

Punctuation Practice: Exercise C[2]

The selection from *A Tale of Two Cities* is shown below, properly capitalized and punctuated. Encourage students to copy the excerpt, not just insert commas into the reprinted paragraph. Copy work is a valuable exercise.

It was the best of times, it was the worst of times, it was the age of wisdom, it was the age of foolishness, it the epoch of belief, it was the epoch of incredulity, it was the season of light, it was the season of darkness, it was the spring of hope, it was the winter of despair, we had everything before us, we had nothing before us, we were all going direct to Heaven, we were all going direct the other way--in short, the period was so far like the present period, that some of its noisiest authorities insisted on its being received, for good or for evil, in the superlative degree of comparison only.

Punctuation Practice: Exercise D[3]

The selection from *Pride and Prejudice* is shown below, properly capitalized and punctuated. Encourage students to copy the excerpt, not just insert commas into the reprinted paragraph. Copy work is a valuable exercise.

"Do you talk by rule, then, while you are dancing?"

"Sometimes. One must speak a little, you know. It would look odd to be entirely silent for half an hour together; and yet for the advantage of *some,* conversation ought to be so arranged, as that they may have the trouble of saying as little as possible."

"Are you consulting your own feelings in the present case, or do you imagine that you are gratifying mine?"

"Both," replied Elizabeth archly; "for I have always seen a great similarity in the turn of our minds."

---

[2] Note: This exercise is provided as a supplement. It did not appear in the original *Mother Tongue Book II*.

[3] Note: This exercise is provided as a supplement. It did not appear in the original *Mother Tongue Book II*.

Punctuation Practice: Exercise E[4]

The following excerpted dialogue, which is taken from Anna Sewell's *Black Beauty*, is shown with proper punctuation and capitals. Encourage students to copy the excerpt, not just insert commas into the reprinted paragraph. Copy work is a valuable exercise.

"Yes, she said; "he is really quite a beauty, and he has such a sweet, good-tempered face, and such a fine, intelligent eye. What do you say to calling him 'Black Beauty'?"

"Black Beauty--why, yes, I think that is a very good name. If you like, it shall be his name." And so it was.

When John went into the stable, he told James that master and mistress had chosen a good, sensible English name for me, that meant something; not like Marengo, or Pegasus, or Abdallah.

Why do you think there is a semicolon placed after *something*? **This semicolon sets off the final clause, which** **contains a list set off by commas. See *Appendix F in* The Mother Tongue: Adapted for Modern Students.**

They both laughed; and James said, "If it was not for bringing back the past, I should have named him Rob Roy, for I never saw two horses more alike."

Punctuation Practice: Exercise F[5]

The following selection, which is taken from Mark Twain's *The Celebrated Jumping Frog of Calaberas County*, is shown with proper punctuation. Encourage students to copy the excerpt, not just insert commas into the reprinted paragraph. Copy work is a valuable exercise.

He never smiled, he never frowned, he never changed his voice from the gentle-flowing key to which he tuned the initial sentence, he never betrayed the slightest suspicion of enthusiasm; but all through the interminable narrative, there ran a vein of impressive earnestness and sincerity, which showed me plainly that so far from his imagining that there was anything ridiculous or funny about his story, he regarded it as a really important matter, and admired its two heroes as men of transcendent genius in *finesse*.

---

[4] Note: This exercise is provided as a supplement. It did not appear in the original *Mother Tongue Book II*.

[5] Note: This exercise is provided as a supplement. It did not appear in the original *Mother Tongue Book II*.

Final Review: Exercise A

Students were instructed to analyze the following sentences by labeling the subject, verb, objects and modifiers. They were to mark clauses with brackets and phrases with parentheses and identify their function in the sentence (adverbial, adjective, object, etc.).[6] They do not need to identify the individual parts of prepositional phrases, unless instructed otherwise. Additional thinking questions are given for the student to answer, or for discussion.

1. They (**S**) (have lighted) (**V**) the (**Adj**) islands (**DO**) (with ruin's torch) (**Adverbial phrase**). *(Thomas Campbell (1777-1844), "Reullura")*
    a. What is the verb tense and voice of *have lighted*? **Perfect tense, active voice**
    b. What kind of phrase is *with ruin's torch*? **Adverbial prepositional phrase**
    c. What does it modify? **have lighted**

2. A (**Adj**) row (**S**) (of tall Lombardy poplars) (**Adjective phrase modifying** *row*) guarded (**V**) the (**Adj**) western (**Adj**) side (**DO**) (of the old mansion) (**Adjective phrase modifying** *side*).
    a. What is the verb tense and voice of *guarded*? **Preterite (past), active voice**
    b. Rewrite the sentence with all modifying words and phrases **removed** (except articles): **A row guarded the side.**
    c. Change the sentence by adding in your own modifiers, but keeping the same pattern of sentence: **Answers will vary. For example:** *A row of armored soldiers guarded the southern side of the stone castle.* **Be sure that they kept the original pattern, "A row-(adjective *of*-phrase)-guarded-(adjective modifier of DO)-the side-(adjective *of*-phrase modifying DO)"**
    d. Did you change the meaning of the sentence entirely? **Answers will vary.**

3. The (**Adj**) geologist (**S**) says (**V**) [that (**C**) a (**Adj**) glacier (**S**) resembles (**V**) a (**Adj**) river (**DO**) (in many respects) (**Adverbial phrase modifying** *resembles*)] (**Subordinate clause is the object of** *says*).
    a. Is this a direct or indirect statement? **Indirect**
    b. Explain the function of *that* in this sentence (see chapter 140). **The conjunction *that* introduces the substantive clause which is reporting the words of the geologist and is the object of *says*.**

4. [Though (**C**) many (**Adj**) years (**S**) (have elapsed) (**V**) since (**Adv**) I (**S**) trod (**V**) the (**Adj**) drowsy (**Adj**) shades (**DO**) (of Sleepy Hollow) (**Adjective phrase**)], I (**S**) question (**V**) [whether (**C**) I (**S**) should (**V**) not (**Adv**) still (**Adv**) find (**V**) the (**Adj**) same (**Adj**) trees (**DO**) and (**C**) the (**Adj**) same (**Adj**) families (**DO**) (vegetating (**participle modifying** *families*) (in its sheltered bosom) (**Adverbial phrase modifying** *vegetating*))] (**subordinate clause is the object of** *question*)].
    (Washington Irving (1783-1859), "The Legend of Sleepy Hollow")
    a. What is the potential verb phrase in this complex sentence? **should find**
    b. *Though many years have elapsed since I trod the drowsy shades of Sleepy Hollow* is classified as what kind of clause? (See chapter 136.) **Concessive clause**
    c. Sometimes sentences beginning with this sort of clause are in the subjunctive mood (see chapters 129-132). Do you think this sentence is in the subjunctive? **No**
    d. Why or why not? **Although the clause is introduced by *though*, the concessive clause is expressed as fact, not supposition. See Section 563 in the text.**

---

[6] Final review sentences are taken from *The Mother Tongue Book II Revised Edition,* © 1908. The additional questions about each sentence have been added by the editors.

5. I (**S**) think (**V**) [that (**C**) I (**S**) have (**V**) not (**Adv**) yet (**Adv**) told (**V**) you (**IO**) [how (**Adv**) we (**S**) left (**V**) that (**Adj**) charming (**Adj**) place (**DO**), Genoa (**App Adj**)] (**DO clause of** *told*)] (**DO clause of** *think*). *Thomas Gray (1716-1771), "Letter to Mr. West")*
    a. What is the appositive in this sentence and what noun does it modify? **Genoa. It modifies** *place.*
    b. How is the phrase *that charming place, Genoa* functioning in the sentence? **It is the direct object of** *left.*
    c. How is the clause *how we left that charming place, Genoa* functioning in the sentence? **It is the direct object of** *told.*

6. The (**Adj**) rain (**S**) swept (**V**) down (**Adv**) (from the half-seen hills) (**Adverbial phrase modifying** *swept*), wreathed (**V**) the (**Adj**) wooded (**Adj**) peaks (**DO**) (with a gray garment) (**Adv phrase**) (of mist) (**Adj phrase modifying** *garment*), and (**C**) filled (**V**) the (**Adj**) valley (**DO**) (with a whitish cloud) (**Adverbial phrase modifying** *filled*).
    a. Is this a simple, compound, or complex sentence? **Simple**
    b. There are three verbs. List them and tell if they are transitive or intransitive. **swept (intransitive), wreathed (transitive), filled (transitive)**
    c. Why is *down* an adverb and not a preposition in this instance? *Down* **has no object and modifies the verb** *swept.* **Ask, "Swept how? Swept down."**

7. [If (**C**) the (**Adj**) whole (**Adj**) world (**S**) (should agree) (**V**) [that (**C**) (*yes and no*) (**S phrase**) (should change) (**V**) their (**Adj**) meanings (**DO**)] (**DO clause of** *should agree*)] (**Conditional clause**), *yes* (**S**) (would deny) (**V**), and *no* (**S**) (would affirm) (**V**). *(Joshua Reynolds (1723-1792), "The Idler")*
    a. This sentence begins with *If*. What are these kinds of sentences called? **Conditional and potential sentences. See chapters 128, 129 and 131.**
    b. Write the main clause here: *Yes* **would deny, and** *no* **would affirm.**
    c. What is the sentence's mood? **Potential mood. See chapter 128, especially the final example in Section 542.**

8. One (**S**) (of the company) (**Adjective phrase**) remarked (**V**) [that (**C**) prudence (**S**) (should be distinguished) (**V phrase**) (from fear) (**Adverbial phrase**)] (**DO clause of** *remarked*). *(Samuel Johnson (1709-1784), "To The Rambler")*
    a. What is the simple subject and predicate of the main clause? **One remarked.**
    b. What is the simple subject and predicate of the subordinate clause? **Prudence should be distinguished.**
    c. What is the mood of the subordinate clause's verb phrase? **Subjunctive mood**

9. The (**Adj**) dry (**Adj**) basin (**S**) (of a fountain) (**Adj phrase modifying** *basin*), and (**C**) a (**Adj**) few (**Adj**) trees (**S**), ragged (**Adj**) and (**C**) unpruned (**Adj**), indicate (**V**) [that (**C**) this (**Adj**) spot (**S**), (in past days) (**Adv phrase**), was (**V**) a (**Adj**) pleasant (**Adj**), shady (**Adj**) retreat (**PN**), filled (**participle modifying** *filled*) (with fruits and flowers and a sweet murmur (of waters)) (**object of** *retreat*)] (**DO clause of** *indicate*). *(Fitz-James O'Brien (1828-1862), "What Was It?")*
    a. How does chapter 101, section 428 describe a participle? **The participle is a verb form which has no subject, but which, partaking of the nature of an adjective, expresses action or state in such a way as to describe or limit a substantive.**
    b. Write the participle phrase that describes *retreat*. *filled with fruits and flowers and a sweet murmur of waters.*
    c. What clause functions as the direct object of *indicate? that this spot, in past days, was a pleasant, shady retreat, filled with fruits and flowers and a sweet murmur of waters.*

10. An (**Adj**) ancient (**Adj**) writer (**S**) reports (**V**) [that (**C**) the (**Adj**) sum (**S**) (of Persian education) (**Adj phrase**) consisted (**V**) (in (teaching the youth (to ride), (to shoot) (with the bow), and (to speak) the truth) (**prepositional adverbial phrase modifying** *consisted*)] (**subordinate clause functioning as the object of** *reports*) . *(Samuel Johnson (1709-1784), "To The Rambler")*

    a.   List the infinitives. **to ride, to shoot, to speak**

    b.   Write the preposition phrase that begins with the preposition *in* and label its parts. **In teaching the youth to ride, to shoot with the bow, and to speak the truth.**

    c.   Write the phrase that is the object of the preposition *in.* **teaching the youth to ride, to shoot with the bow, and to speak the truth.**

    d.   The participle *teaching* takes three objects. What are the three object phrases? **(to ride), (to shoot with the bow), and (to speak the truth)**

    e.   What is the function of *the youth* in this sentence? **It is the indirect object of the participle** *teaching.*

    f.   Which infinitive takes an object? What is the object of this infinitive? *To speak* **takes the object** *truth.*

Final Review: Exercise B

Students were instructed to analyze the following sentences by labeling the subject, verb, objects and modifiers. They were to mark clauses with brackets and phrases with parentheses and identify their function in the sentence (adverbial, adjective, object, etc.).[7] They do not need to identify the individual parts of prepositional phrases, unless instructed otherwise. Additional thinking questions are given for the student to answer, or for discussion.

1. Those (**S**) [who (**S**) (in their lives) (**Adv**) (were applauded) (**V**) and (**C**) admired (**V**)] (**relative clause modifying** *those*), are (**V**) sometimes (**Adv**) laid (**V**) (at last) (**Adv phrase**) (in the ground) (**Adv phrase**) (without the common honor) (**Adv phrase**) (of a stone) (**Adj phrase modifying** *stone*).
   a. What is the simple subject and predicate of this sentence? **Those are laid.**
   b. Write the relative clause that modifies the pronoun *Those*. **Who in their lives were applauded and admired**
   c. Is it restrictive or descriptive? **Restrictive**

2. Betrayed (**Adj**), deserted (**Adj**), disorganized (**Adj**), unprovided (**Adj**) (with resources) (**Adv phrase modifying** *unprovided*), begirt (**Adj**) (with enemies) (**Adv phrase modifying** *begirt*), the (**Adj**) whole (**Adj**) city (**S**) was (**V**) still (**Adv**) no (**Adj modifying** *conquest*) easy (**Adj**) conquest (**PN**). *(Lord Thomas Macaulay (1800-1859), History of England)*
   a. List the participles. **Betrayed, deserted, disorganized, unprovided, begirt**
   b. What substantive do the participles modify adjectively? *City*

3. The (**Adj**) progress (**S**) (of agriculture) (**Adj phrase**) (has led) (**V**) (to (the draining of mosses) (**OP** *to*), (the felling (of forests)) (**OP** *to*), and (**C**) (the (**Adj**) transformation (of heaths and wastes) (**Adj prep phrase modifying** *transformation*) (into arable land) (**Adj prep phrase modifying** *transformation*)) (**OP** *to*)) (**Adv prepositional phrase modifying** *has led*). *(Sir Archibald Geikie (1835-1924), "Landscape in History")*
   a. What is the simple subject and predicate of this sentence? **Progress has led.**
   b. Is this a simple, compound, or complex sentence? **Simple**
   c. Are the words *draining* and *felling* participles or verbal nouns (gerunds)? Why? **Verbal nouns (gerunds) These participles are substantives in this sentence, the objects of the preposition** *to*.
   d. The preposition *to* has multiple objects. What are they? **draining, felling, transformation**
   e. List the prepositional phrases. (**of agriculture**), (**to the draining (of mosses), (the felling (of forests)), and the transformation (of heaths and wastes)**), (**into arable land**). *Note that several phrases are nested within the bigger prepositional phrase.*

4. The (**Adj**) autumn (**Adj**) wind (**S**) wandered (**V**) (among the branches) (**Adv phrase**). It (**S**) whirled (**V**) away (**Adv**) the (**Adj**) leaves (**DO**) (from all) (**Adv phrase**) (except the pine-trees) (**Adj modifying** *all*), and (**C**) moaned (**V**) [(as if) (**C**) it (**S**) lamented (**V**) the (**Adj**) desolation (**DO**) [which (**relative pronoun, object of** *caused*) it (**S**) caused (**V**)]] (**subordinate adverbial clause modifying** *moaned*). *(Nathaniel Hawthorne (1804-1864), "The Gentle Boy") Note: In this sentence it functions as a pronoun (substantive) with the antecedent* wind.
   a. Write the simple subject and predicate of both sentences. **Wind wandered. It whirled and moaned.**
   b. Is the second sentence a simple, compound, or complex sentence? **complex**
   c. Write the simple subject and predicate of the subordinate clause that modifies *moaned*. **It lamented. (See chapter 139.)**
   d. Write the subordinate clause that modifies *desolation*. **Which it caused.**

---

[7] Final review sentences are taken from *The Mother Tongue Book II Revised Edition*, © 1908. The additional questions about each sentence have been added by the editors.

5. (Beneath the shelter) (of one hut) (**Adv phrase**), (in the bright blaze) (**Adv phrase**) (of the same fire) (**Adj phrase modifying** *blaze*), sat (**V**) this (**Adj**) varied (**Adj**) group (**S**) (of adventurers) (**Adj phrase modifying** *group*). *(Nathaniel Hawthorne (1804-1864), "The Great Carbuncle")*

   a. Write the simple subject and predicate. **Group sat.**

   b. Why do you think the author inverted the order of this sentence, placing the predicate first? **Answers will vary. By placing the predicate before the subject, and by placing two adverbial phrases before it, the author builds suspense.**

   c. Write a sentence in the same pattern, with the same subject and verb, but create your own adverbial and adjective phrases. Here is the pattern:
   (Adverbial phrase with adjective phrase)-(Adverbial phrase with adjective phrase)-(**sat**)-(Adjective-Adjective-**group**)-(Adjective phrase)
   Answers will vary. Look for something such as this (parentheses shown to make the elements clearer): (Around the table) (of her kitchen), (with a full tray) (of chocolate cookies), (sat) (her regular group) (of friends).

6. One (**S**) gains (**V**) nothing (**DO**) (by attempting (to shut) out the sprites (of the weather)) (**adverbial prepositional phrase modifying** *gains*).

   They (**S**) come (**V**) in (at the keyhole) (**Adv phrase**); they (**S**) peer (**V**) (through the dripping panes) (**Adv phrase**); they (**S**) insinuate (**V**) themselves (**DO**) (through the crevices) (**Adv phrase modifying** *insinuate*) (of the casement) (**Adj phrase modifying** *casement*), or (**C**) plump (**V**) themselves (**DO**) (down the chimney) (**Adv phrase**) astride (**Adv**) (of the raindrops) (**Adv phrase modifying** *astride*).

   (John Greenleaf Whittier (1807-1892), "Yankee Gypsies")

   a. Write the simple subject, predicate and object of the first sentence. **One gains nothing.**

   b. The second sentence is compound. List the pairs of subjects and verbs for each independent clause. **They come; they peer; they insinuate or plump.**

   c. List any participles, infinitives, and verbal nouns and write their part of speech in the sentences (e.g. adjective, object, etc.) **Attempting: object of the preposition** *by*; **to shut: object of the verbal noun** *attempting*; **dripping: adjective modifying** *panes*

7. (Miss Jessie Brown) (**S**) was (**V**) ten (**Adj**) years (**Adverbial objective**) younger (**Pred Adj**) [than (**C**) her (**Adj**) sister (**S**) *was* (**the verb is omitted in this adverbial clause of comparison**)], and (**C**) twenty (**Adj**) shades (**Adverbial objective**) prettier (**Pred Adj**). *Note: Refer to chapter 117, Section 498 and note for help with adverbial objectives (nouns that modify verbs or adjectives in an adverbial way).*

   a. Write the adjectives of comparison. **younger; prettier**

   b. Are they the comparative or superlative degree? **comparative**

   c. This sentence is an elliptical sentence (see chapter 143). What are the missing words and where should they go? **Miss Jessie Brown was ten years younger than her sister <u>was</u>, and <u>she was</u> twenty shades prettier.**

8. How (**Adv**) few (**S**) appear (**V**) (in those streets) (**Adv phrase**) [which (**S**) but (**Adv**) some (**Adv**) few (**Adj**) hours (**Adverbial objective**) ago (**Adv**) (were crowded) (**V phrase**)]!

   a. The subordinate clause begins with the relative pronoun *which*. What is its antecedent? **Streets**

   b. Can you tell what kind of phrase *but some few hours ago* is? **Adverbial objective (See chapter 117) modifying** *were crowded*.

   c. The word *few* appears twice in this sentence. What is the part of speech of *few* in each instance? **The first** *few* **is the subject of the sentence; the second** *few* **is an adjective modifying** *hours*.

9. (From these quiet windows) (**Adv phrase modifying** *looked*) the (**Adj**) figures (**S**) (of passing travelers) (**Adj phrase**) looked (**V**) too (**Adv**) remote (**Adv**) and (**C**) dim (**Adv**) [(to disturb) (**complementary infinitive**) the (**Adj**) sense (**Obj of infinitive**) (of privacy) (**Adj modifying** *sense*)] (**infinitive phrase modifying** *remote* **and** *dim*).

    a. Write the simple subject and predicate. **Figures looked.**
    b. What is the function of the infinitive phrase *to disturb the sense of privacy*? **Complementary infinitive of purpose (See chapter 127)**
    c. Does the infinitive *to disturb* take an object? If so, what is it? **Yes,** *the sense of privacy*

10. There (**Adv**) is (**V**) exquisite (**Adj**) delight (**S**) [(in picking up for one's self an arrowhead) [that was dropped centuries ago and has never been handled since] (**subordinate adjective clause modifying** *arrowhead*)] (**Predicate nominative substantive phrase and clause**).

    a. What is the subject of this sentence? *Delight.* **The adverb** *there* **is an expletive in this sentence. (See "Extra Resources: Miscellaneous Idioms" at the end of Workbook 2. See also Section 536 in** *The Mother Tongue: Adapted for Modern Students.***)**
    b. Read the "Extra Resources: Miscellaneous Idioms" chapter in this workbook. Explain why *there* is not the subject and tell what *there* is called when used in this way. **The adverb** *there* **is called an expletive; it has no meaning in the sentence.**
    c. What is the other pronoun that is often used in English as a filler, just as *there*? **It**
    d. Is the demonstrative *that* used substantively as a pronoun or as an adjective in this sentence? **Substantively as a pronoun with** *arrowhead* **as the antecedent.**

Final Review: Exercise C

Students were instructed to analyze the following sentences by labeling the subject, verb, objects and modifiers. They were to mark clauses with brackets and phrases with parentheses and identify their function in the sentence (adverbial, adjective, object, etc.).[8] They do not need to identify the individual parts of prepositional phrases, unless instructed otherwise. Additional thinking questions are given for the student to answer, or for discussion.

1. Sea (**Adj**) air (**S**) ripens (**V**) friendship (**DO**) quicker (**Adv**) (than the hotbed of a city [ripens]) (**Adverbial clause of comparison-see chapter 139**) .
   a. What two groups of words are connected by the preposition *than*? (**Sea air ripens friendship quicker**) **and** (**the hotbed of a city**)
   b. What two settings are being compared in this sentence? *Sea air* **and** *the hotbed of a city*
   c. Write your own sentence telling what you think "...ripens friendship quicker than..." **Answers will vary.**

2. The (**Adj**) weather (**S**) was (**V**) so (**Adv**) bad (**Adj**) [that (**C**) I (**S**) could (**V**) not (**Adv**) embark (**V**) (that (**Adj**) night) (**Adverbial objective modifier-See chapter 117**)](**Subordinate adverbial clause**).
   a. The demonstrative *that* is used twice in this sentence. How is each one used? As a conjunction? Substantively as a pronoun? Or adjectively? Give your reasons. **The first *that* is a conjunction connecting the subordinate clause *I could not embark that night* to the main clause. The second *that* is an adjective modifying the noun *night*.**
   b. Refer to chapters 134-137 and classify the subordinate clause. **Clause of result.**

3. Amsterdam (**S**) was (**V**) the (**Adj**) place (**PN**) [where (**relative/conjunctive adverb**) the (**Adj**) leading (**participle modifying *Scotch and English***) (Scotch and English) (**S phrase**) assembled (**V**)] (**Adverbial clause modifying *place***). (*Lord Thomas Macaulay (1800-1859)*, History of England)
   a. List the proper nouns. **Amsterdam, Scotch, English**
   b. Rewrite this as a simple sentence without losing any meaning. **The leading Scotch and English assembled in Amsterdam.**

4. He (**S**) shouts (**V**) [(as if) (**C**) he (**S**) (were trying) (**V phrase**) his (**Adj**) voice (**DO**) (against a northwest gale of wind) (**Adv phrase modifying *were trying***)] (**Adverbial clause modifying *shouts***). (*Sir Walter Scott (1771-1832)*, The Pirate)
   a. Write the main clause. **He shouts.**
   b. Is the subordinate clause an adverbial or adjective clause? **Adverbial**
   c. What is the verb tense and number of *shouts?* **Present tense, singular.**
   d. What is the verb tense and number of *were trying*? **Past (preterite) progressive, passive, singular**
   e. What is the mood of the main clause? **Indicative mood.**
   f. What is the mood of the subordinate clause? **Subjunctive. See chapter 131, Section 567.**

5. (Captain Brown and Miss Jenkyns) (**S phrase**) were (**V**) not (**Adv**) very (**Adv**) cordial (**PA**) (to each other) (**Adv phrase**). (*Elizabeth Cleghorn Gaskell (1810-1865)*, Cranford)
   a. What kind of pronoun is *each other*? **Compound pronoun (see Section 356)**
   b. Is it a substantive or adjective in this sentence? **Substantive, the object of the preposition *to*.**

6. (For a moment) (**Adverbial phrase modifying *in jeopardy***) his (**Adj**) life (**S**) was (**V**) (in jeopardy) (**Pred Adj**).
   a. Parse the pronoun *his*, giving the gender, number, and case. **Masculine, singular, possessive/genitive**

---

[8] Final review sentences are taken from *The Mother Tongue Book II Revised Edition,* © 1908. The additional questions about each sentence have been added by the editors.

    b.   Write the phrases and tell what their part of speech in the sentence is. **(For a moment) - adverbial phrase; (in jeopardy) - predicate adjective**

7.   Martha (**S**) was (**V**) blunt (**Pred Adj**) and (**C**) plain-spoken (**Pred Adj**) (to a fault) (**Adv phrase modifying** *plain-spoken*). *(Elizabeth Cleghorn Gaskell (1810-1865),* Cranford*)*

    a.   Why is *plain-spoken* hyphenated? **This is a compound adjective modifying** *Martha.*

    b.   What kind of verb is *was* in this sentence? **A linking verb or** *copula.* **See chapter 10.**

8.   The (**Adj**) old (**Adj**) man (**S**) (had become) (**V**) sluggish (**Pred Adj**) and (**C**) self-indulgent (**Pred Adj**).

    a.   Write the simple subject and predicate. **Man had become.**

    b.   Parse the verb phrase and give its tense, person, and number. **Had become, pluperfect, active voice, third person, singular.**

    c.   Is the verb phrase transitive or intransitive? **Intransitive**

9.   The (**Adj**) major (**S**) had (**V**) a (**Adj**) wiry, (**Adj**) well-trained, (**Adj**) elastic (**Adj**) figure (**DO**), a (**Adj**) stiff (**Adj**) military (**Adj**) throw-back (**DO**) (of his head) (**Adj phrase modifying** *throw-back*), and (**C**) a (**Adj**) springing (**participle adjective**) step (**DO**). *(Elizabeth Cleghorn Gaskell (1810-1865), adapted from* Cranford*)*

    a.   Parse the verb phrase and give its tense, person, and number. **had, preterite past, third person, singular**

    b.   Is the verb phrase transitive or intransitive? **Transitive**

    c.   List the three direct objects. **figure, throw-back, step**

10. The (**Adj**) traveler (**S**) quickened (**V**) his (**Adj**) pace (**DO**) [when (**Adv**) he (**S**) reached (**V**) the (**Adj**) outskirts (**DO**) (of the town) (**Adj phrase modifying** *outskirts*)] (**Adverbial clause modifying** *quickened*), [for (**C**) a (**Adj**) gloomy (**Adj**) extent (**S**) (of nearly four miles) (**Adj phrase modifying** *extent*) lay (**V**) (between him and his home) (**Adv phrase modifying** *lay*)] (**Subordinate causal clause**). *(Nathaniel Hawthorne (1804-1864), "The Gentle Boy")*

    a.   There are four pronouns in this sentence. Parse them by giving their gender, number, and case.

        1) his: masculine, singular, genitive (possessive)

        2) he: masculine, singular, nominative

        3) him: masculine, singular, objective

        4) his: masculine, singular, genitive (possessive)

    b.   Is this a compound, complex, or compound-complex sentence? Why? **Compound-complex. It is a compound sentence and the first independent clause contains a subordinate clause.**

Final Review: Exercise D

Students were instructed to analyze the following sentences by labeling the subject, verb, objects and modifiers. They were to mark clauses with brackets and phrases with parentheses and identify their function in the sentence (adverbial, adjective, object, etc.).[9] They do not need to identify the individual parts of prepositional phrases, unless instructed otherwise. Additional thinking questions are given for the student to answer, or for discussion.

1. The (**Adj**) conversation (**S**) (of the passengers) (**Adj phrase modifying** *conversation*) (in the coach) (**Adj phrase modifying** *passengers*) was (**V**) gay (**Pred Adj**) and (**C**) animated (**Pred Adj**).
   a. Rewrite the sentence, replacing the *of*-phrase with the genitive and keeping the meaning intact. **The passenger's conversation in the coach was gay and animated.**
   b. Rewrite the sentence, but this time make *passengers* the subject and use *conversed* as the verb. What must you do to *gay* and *animated*? **The passengers in the coach conversed gaily and with animation.** *Gay* **was changed to an adverb form and** *animated* **was placed in a prepositional phrase.**

2. The (**Adj**) silver (**Adj**) light (**S**), (with quivering glance) (**Adj phrase modifying** *light*),
   Played (**S**) (on the water's expanse) (**Adv phrase modifying** *played*). (*Sir Walter Scott (1771-1832), "Lady of the Lake"*)
   a. What is the simple subject and simple predicate? **Light played.**
   b. Write a new sentence, following the same pattern, but use "*Leaves rustled*" as the simple subject and predicate. **Answers will vary. Possible suggestion:** *The dead leaves, with redding shades, Rustled in the wind's waves.*
   c. Write a new sentence, following the same pattern, but use "*Sound echoed*" as the simple subject and predicate. **Answers will vary. Possible suggestion:** *The crystal sound, with ringing call, Echoed in the castle's hall.*

3. The (**Adj**) appearance (**S**) (of Rip) (**Adj phrase modifying** *appearance*), (with his long grizzled beard, his rusty fowling piece, his uncouth dress, and the army of women and children [that had gathered at his heels] (**Adj clause modifying** *children*)) (**Adj prepositional phrase modifying** *Rip*), soon (**Adv**) attracted (**V**) the (**Adj**) attention (**DO**) (of the tavern politicians) (**Adj phrase modifying** *attention*). *Note: *Students aren't required to identify all the parts of the prepositional phrases.*
   (*Washington Irving (1783-1859), "Rip Van Winkle"*)
   a. What is the simple subject and simple predicate? **Appearance attracted.**
   b. What are the objects of the preposition *with*? **beard, piece, dress, army**

4. Nature (**S**) never (**Adv**) hurries (**V**). (Atom by atom) (**Adv phrase**), (little by little) (**Adv phrase**), she (**S**) achieves (**V**) her (**Adj**) work (**DO**). (*Ralph Waldo Emerson (1803-1882), "Farming"*)
   a. What word do you think the idiomatic phrases *Atom by atom* and *little by little* modify? **Achieves**
   b. Parse the pronouns *she* and *her*, giving their gender, number, and case. **F, S, N; F, S, G**
   c. What is the antecedent? **Nature**
   d. What kind of noun (common or proper, abstract or concrete) is *Nature*? **Common, abstract.**

5. The (**Adj**) sky (**S**) was (**V**) clear (**Pred Adj**), and (**C**) a (**Adj**) single (**Adj**) star (**S**) shown (**V**) out (**Adv**) sharply (**Adv**).
   a. Is this sentence compound, complex, or compound-complex? Why? **Compound. It is two independent clauses linked with a conjunction.**

---

[9] Final review sentences are taken from *The Mother Tongue Book II Revised Edition*, © 1908. The additional questions about each sentence have been added by the editors.

b.   Parse the verbs and give their tense, number, and tell if they are transitive or intransitive. **was: past, singular, intransitive. shown: past, singular, intransitive**

6.   Fast (**PA**) are (**V**) the (**Adj**) flying (**Participle Adj**) moments (**S**), faster (**PA**) are (**V**) the (**Adj**) hoofs (**S**) (of our horses) (**Adj phrase modifying** *hoofs*). *(Thomas De Quincey (1785-1859), "The English Mail-Coach")*

a.   What are the degrees of comparison for the adjectives? **fast: positive; faster: comparative;**

b.   Identify the words used in alliteration. **fast, flying, faster; hoofs, horses**

7.   We (**S**) trod (**V**) the (**Adj**) fire (**DO**) out (**Adv**), locked (**V**) the (**Adj**) door (**DO**), and (**C**) set (**V**) forth (**Adv**) (upon our walk) (**Adv**). *(Robert Louis Stevenson (1850-1894),* Kidnapped*)*

a.   List the simple subject and simple predicates. **We trod, locked, and set.**

b.   Parse the verbs and give their tense, voice (active or passive), person, and number. **trod, locked, set: past, active, first, plural**

8.   No (**Adv**) man's (**Adj**) power (**S**) (can be) (**V phrase**) equal (**PA**) (to his will) (**Adj phrase**). *(Samuel Johnson (1709-1784), "To The Rambler")*

a.   What kind of verb phrase is *can be*? **Potential (chapter 128)**

b.   What is the past form of *can*? **could**

c.   What is the meaning of *can* and *may*? *Can:* **ability,** *may:* **permission**

9.   Everything (**S**) (which (**Relative pronoun S**) helps (**V**) a (**Adj**) boy's (**Adj**) power (**DO**) (of observation) (**Adj**)), helps (**V**) his (**Adj**) power (**DO**) (of learning) (**Adj**).

a.   List the substantives and identify their case (nominative, genitive, objective). **everything: N; boy's: G; power: O; observation: O; power: O**

b.   Is *which* a descriptive or restrictive relative pronoun (see chapter 121)? **Restrictive**

10. [While (**Adv**) many (**Adv**) a (**Adj**) thoughtless (**Adj**) person (**S**) (is whirled) (**V phrase**) (through Europe) (**Adv phrase**) (without gaining a single idea) (**Adv participle phrase modifying** *is whirled*)] (**Adverbial clause of time**), the (**Adj**) observing (**Participle adjective**) eye (**S**) and (**C**) inquiring (**Participle adjective**) mind (**S**) find (**V**) matter (**DO**) (of improvement and delight) (**Adj phrase modifying** *matter*) (in every ramble) (**Adv phrase modifying** *find*)). *(Charles Kingsley (1819-1875), "Lecture at Wellington College")*

a.   Write the participles and explain their function in the sentence. **gaining: verbal noun, object of** *without;* **observing: adjective; inquiring: adjective**

b.   Refer to chapters 134-139 and identify the category of the subordinate clause in this sentence. **Adverbial clause of time.**

Final Review: Exercise E

Students were instructed to analyze the following sentences by labeling the subject, verb, objects and modifiers. They were to mark clauses with brackets and phrases with parentheses and identify their function in the sentence (adverbial, adjective, object, etc.).[10] They do not need to identify the individual parts of prepositional phrases, unless instructed otherwise. Additional thinking questions are given for the student to answer, or for discussion.

1. ((Sweet smiling village), (loveliest of the lawn) (**Appositive phrase modifying** *village*)), (**Vocative**) Thy (**Adj**) sports (**S**) (are fled) (**V phrase**), and (**C**) all (**Adj**) thy (**Adj**) charms (**S**) withdrawn (**V**). (*Oliver Goldsmith (1730-1774), "The Deserted Village"*)
   a. What is the phrase "sweet smiling village, loveliest of the lawn," called in this sentence? **vocative**
   b. How should it be treated in analysis? **It should be marked as vocative; it is not the subject.**

2. The (**Adj**) bristling (**Adj**) burdock (**S**), the (**Adj**) sweet-scented (**Adj**) catnip (**S**), and (**C**) the (**Adj**) humble (**Adj**) yarrow (**S**) planted (**V**) themselves (**DO**) (along the woodland road) (**Adv phrase**). (*Henry David Thoreau (1817-1862), "A Week on the Concord and Merrimack Rivers"*)
   a. What is the self-pronoun in this sentence? **themselves**
   b. Is it an intensive pronoun or an object? **object**

3. [You] (**S**) Be (**V**) just (**PA**) and (**C**) [you] (**S**) fear (**V**) not (**Adv**). *Note: Students need to supply the subject* **you.** *(William Shakespeare (1564-1616),* Henry VIII)
   a. Is this a declarative, imperative, or interrogative sentence? **imperative**
   b. What is the second person indicative form of the verb *to be*? *are*
   c. Why is it *be* in this sentence? **The imperative mood (chapter 115, Section 485) form of the verb** *to be* **is** *be.*

4. Fear (**S**) makes (**V**) man (**DO**) a (**Adj**) slave (**Pred Obj**) (to others) (**Adj phrase modifying** *slave*). *(William Ellery Channing (1780-1842))*
   a. Is *fear* an abstract or concrete noun? **abstract**
   b. Refer to chapter 118. Why is *slave* a predicate objective (also called a complementary object)? *Slave* **is like a second object of the verb** *makes*, **completing the sense of the predicate. It is called a predicate objective, or complementary object.**

5. He (**S**) [who (**Relative pronoun S**) plants (**V**) a (**Adj**) tree (**DO**)] (**Restrictive clause**) plants (**V**) a (**Adj**) hope (**DO**). *(Lucy Larcom (1824-1893), "Plant a Tree")*
   a. Write the main clause. **He plants a hope.**
   b. Write the subordinate clause. **Who plants a tree**
   c. What is the relative pronoun? **who**   What is its function in the clause? *Who* **is the subject of the restrictive clause.**

6. The (**Adj**) birds (**S**) (were hopping and twittering) (**V phrase**) (among the bushes) (**Adv phrase**), and (**C**) the (**Adj**) eagle (**S**) (was wheeling) (**V phrase**) aloft (**Adv**) and (**C**) breasting (**V**) the (**Adj**) pure (**Adj**) mountain (**Adj**) breeze (**DO**). *(Washington Irving (1783-1859), "Rip Van Winkle")*
   a. Write the verbs and parse them, giving their tense, person, and number. *were hopping*: **past progressive, third, plural;** *were twittering*: **past progressive, third, plural;** *was wheeling*: **past progressive, third, singular;** *was breasting*: **past progressive, third, singular**

---

[10] Final review sentences are taken from *The Mother Tongue Book II Revised Edition*, © 1908. The additional questions about each sentence have been added by the editors.

7. I (**S**) threw (**V**) aside (**Adv**) the (**Adj**) newspaper (**DO**), and (**C**) explored (**V**) my (**Adj**) way (**DO**) (to the kitchen) (**Adj phrase modifying** *way*), [(to take) (**Infinitive**) a (**Adj**) peep (**Obj of infinitive**) (at the group) (**Adj phrase modifying** *peep*) [that (**relative pronoun with** *group* **as antecedent**) seemed (**V**) so (**Adv**) merry (**Adj**)] (**Adjective clause modifying** *group*)] (**Subordinate infinitive clause of purpose telling the purpose of going to the kitchen**). *(Washington Irving (1783-1859), "The Inn Kitchen")*
   a. Rewrite this sentence replacing all the verbs. **Answers will vary. Suggestion:** *I tossed aside the newspaper, and made my way to the kitchen, to sneak a peep at the group that was so merry.*
   b. Write the simple subject and predicate. **I threw and explored.**

8. You (**S**) think (**V**) me (**DO**), (no doubt) (**idiomatic expression and a shortened form of** *there is no doubt about it*), a (**Adj**) tardy (**Adj**) correspondent (**Pred Obj**). *(William Cowper (1731-1800), "Letter to Rev. Walter Bagot")*
   a. Parse each pronoun and give its gender, number, and case. **You: M/F, S, N   me: M/F, S, O**
   b. Why is *correspondent* a predicate objective? Refer to chapter 118. **Verbs of choosing, calling, naming, making, and thinking, may take two objects referring to the same person or thing. The first of these is the direct object, and the second, which completes the sense of the predicate, is called a predicate objective. The predicate objective is often called the complementary object, because it completes the sense of the verb. It is sometimes called the objective attribute. (Section 500)**

9. The (**Adj**) fugitives (**S**) broke (**V**) down (**Adv**) the (**Adj**) bridges (**DO**) and (**C**) burned (**V**) the (**Adj**) ferryboats (**DO**). *(Lord Thomas Macaulay (1800-1859),* History of England*)*
   a. Is *down* an adverb or preposition? **Adverb**
   b. Is this a simple sentence with a compound predicate or a complex sentence? **Simple sentence with compound predicate**

10. Somebody (**S**) tapped (**V**) me (**DO**) (on the shoulder) (**Adv phrase modifying** *tapped*), and (**C**) I (**S**) saw (**V**) a (**Adj**) couple (**DO**) (of rough-looking fellows) (**Adj phrase modifying** *couple*) (behind me) (**Adv phrase modifying** *saw*).
   a. Is this a compound or complex sentence? **Compound**
   b. List the pronouns and give their gender, number, and case. **Somebody: M/F, S, N   me: M/F, S, O   I: M/F, S, N   me: M/F, S, O**

Final Review: Exercise F

Analyze the following sentences by labeling the subject, verb, objects and modifiers. Be sure to mark clauses with brackets and phrases with parentheses and identify their function in the sentence (adverbial, adjective, object, etc.).[11] They do not need to identify the individual parts of prepositional phrases, unless instructed otherwise. Additional thinking questions are given for the student to answer, or for discussion.

Write answers to the thinking questions about each sentence, or discuss orally with your teacher.

1. The (**Adj**) courtyard (**S**) was (**V**) (in an uproar) (**Adv phrase**), the (**Adj**) house (**S**) (in a bustle) (**Adv phrase**). *(Washington Irving (1783-1859), "Tales of a Traveler")*
    a. Is this a simple, compound, or complex sentence? **compound**
    b. What is the verb for the subject *house*? **The verb *was* is omitted.**
    c. What are sentences like this one called? **elliptical sentences**
    d. Review the list of sentences in chapter 143, section 620. Write the sentence that matches this pattern. **His hair was light, his eyes [were] blue.**

2. He (**S**) seldom (**Adv**), [it is true] , sent (**V**) his (**Adj**) eyes (**DO**) or (**C**) his (**Adj**) thoughts (**DO**) (beyond the boundaries) (**Adv phrase modifying** *sent*) (of his own farm) (**Adj phrase modifying** *boundaries*); but (**C**) (within those boundaries) (**Adj phrase modifying** *everything*) everything (**S**) was (**V**) snug (**PA**), happy (**PA**), and (**C**) well-conditioned (**PA**). *(Washington Irving (1783-1859), "The Legend of Sleepy Hollow")* *Note: This clause has the expletive* it *which refers back to the main clause. Compare, "[That] he seldom sent his eyes or his thoughts beyond the boundaries is true.")*
    a. Why is this sentence divided with a semi-colon? **It divides the compound sentence.**
    b. Is this a compound, complex, or compound-complex sentence? Why? **Compound. It contains two independent clauses.**

3. (With rushing winds and gloomy skies) (**Adv phrase modifying** *dies*)
    The (**Adj**) dark (**Adj**) and (**C**) stubborn (**Adj**) winter (**S**) dies (**V**). *(Bayard Taylor (1825-1878), "March!")*
    a. Rewrite this couplet with the complete subject first and the complete predicate second. **The dark and stubborn winter dies with rushing winds and gloomy skies.**
    b. Why do you think the poet chose to divide the predicate? **Answers may vary. Perhaps the poet wanted to create suspense.**

4. [(How many) (**S phrase**) (of the enemy) (**Adj phrase modifying** *how many*) (were taken) (**V phrase**)] (**object clause of the verb** *did know*) he (**S**) did (**V**) not (**Adv**) know (**V**). *Note: If students are confused, try reordering the sentence as follows: "He did not know how many of the enemy were taken."*
    a. Parse *were taken* and give its tense, number, and person. **past passive, singular, third**
    b. What is the subject and its number? **He, singular**
    c. Why isn't this sentence punctuated with a question mark? **This is not asking, *"How many?"*, but is stating that *he did not know how many were taken.***

5. I (**S**) loved (**V**) the (**Adj**) brimming (**Adj**) wave (**DO**) [that (**S**) swam (**V**)
    (Through quiet meadows) (**Adv phrase modifying** *swam*) (round the mill) (**Adv phrase modifying** *swam*)] (**Adj clause modifying** *wave*). *(Alfred, Lord Tennyson (1809-1892), "The Miller's Daughter")*
    a. What kind of clause is the subordinate clause? **Adjective clause modifying** *wave*

---

[11] Final review sentences are taken from *The Mother Tongue Book II Revised Edition*, © 1908. The additional questions about each sentence have been added by the editors.

b. Is the demonstrative *that* used as a conjunction, substantively as a pronoun, or as an adjective? *That* **is a relative pronoun that functions as the subject of** *swam.*

6. The (**Adj**) crows (**S**) (were wheeling) (**V phrase**) (behind the plough) (**Adv phrase modifying** *were wheeling*) (in scattering clusters) (**Adv phrase modifying** *were wheeling*). *(S. R. Crockett (1859-1914), "The Stickit Minister")*
   a. Write the simple subject and predicate. **Crows were wheeling**
   b. Parse the verb phrase by giving its tense, person, and number. **past progressive, third, plural**
   c. Write the participles and tell the function of each one in the sentence. **wheeling: part of the verb phrase; scattering: adjective modifying** *clusters.*

7. History (**S**) informs (**V**) us (**IO**) [that (**C**) Louisiana (**S**) once (**Adv**) belonged (**V**) (to France) (**Adv phrase**)] (**subordinate clause as DO**).
   a. Which nouns are proper nouns? **Louisiana, France**
   b. Which noun is an abstract noun? **History**
   c. What is the function of the subordinate clause in the sentence? **Direct object of** *informs.*

Manufactured by Amazon.ca
Acheson, AB

16664578R00068